THE GREENWOOD HAT

Yours truly
James Anon.

THE
GREENWOOD HAT

BEING

A MEMOIR OF JAMES ANON

1885–1887

BY

J. M. BARRIE

WITH A PREFACE BY

THE EARL BALDWIN OF BEWDLEY, K.G.

LONDON
PETER DAVIES LIMITED

Fifty copies privately printed in 1930
The whole reset and first published, November 1937

Printed in Great₁ Britain for PETER DAVIES LTD. by T. and A. CONSTABLE LTD.
at the University Press, Edinburgh

PREFACE

THIS little book was printed privately a few years ago for some of Barrie's friends, and I rejoice that it is now being given to the world for the delight of those who love the man and his work.

It is an autobiography of early days and early struggles, clear, sharply clear, yet fairy-like and mellowed in that soft autumn light in which Seventy looks back on Twenty-five.

And what treasure is to be found in it! What riddles to be solved!

The happy reader will learn what *was* the Hat and why he bought it.

He will know why Barrie took to smoking. Where else is told the story of the Allahakbarries and who was their dear enemy?

There was only one writer whom Barrie tried to imitate. Who was he?

Who got Barrie on to the Press? You will never guess, so I will tell you. Shakespeare. Yes, but how? And that too you will learn.

Not to weary you, only two or three more questions.

Why at one dinner would Barrie be comparatively bright and at another drearier than ever?

And lastly: with which hand was *Dear Brutus* written, and why? and with which hand *Quality Street*? and what happened to the beautiful copperplate hand of his boyhood? All these things, and "aye lots more," as the old country song has it, are to be found in these pages.

But the Adelphi Ghosts are gone.

The real Bohemia begins in Adelphi Terrace, Barrie tells us, after the last member of the Savage Club has departed for the night. The only club whose ways he really knew was the club of the Adelphi Ghosts: Davy Garrick, Mrs. Bracegirdle, Dr. Johnson, Bozzie, Peter the Great, Pepys, the brothers Adam, Mr. Micawber, the Fat Boy, Charles Lamb, Gibbon and Emma Hart. He knew them all.

Adelphi Terrace is gone: the Ghosts are gone. To those who knew Barrie in his eyry above the Terrace it seemed unthinkable that he would survive the destruction of the Adelphi.

But wherever the Adelphi Ghosts are fled, he will have found Charles Lamb.

BALDWIN OF BEWDLEY.

CONTENTS

ILLUSTRATIONS

CHAPTER I

THIS book consists merely of some old newspaper articles tied together with a string of memories which the re-reading of them has evoked. They are samples of hundreds I wrote (as Mr. Anon) in my first two years in London in the late 'eighties. The newspapers containing them I used to drop in Bloomsbury, leaving them to lie where they fell. They usually fell in Red Lion Street or Lamb's Conduit Street, where I bought the evening journal on which I did precariously subsist, make sure that another article had been at last accepted, and then (as I had no interest in Affairs) drop the journal in any doorway and pass on, suddenly looking not quite so thin.

To be more candid, I question whether I make this memoir of Anon to uplift my friends so much as in idleness to recall myself. I am yielding to sentiment; not as the gentle reader may say (with I hope a tolerant smile) for the first time. I wish it had been left out of me, but there it is. When I was a very small boy, another as small was woeful because he could not join in our rough play

A

lest he damaged the 'mourning blacks' in which he was attired. So I nobly exchanged clothing with him for an hour, and in mine he disported forgetfully while I sat on a stone in his and lamented with tears, though I knew not for whom. It is a recent discovery that is making me, maybe, similarly sentimental over these writings of the past. I don't mean that I have been searching the doorways of Red Lion Street or Lamb's Conduit Street, which are all no doubt now put to other uses. What I mean is that I found a bundle of withered articles unexpectedly in an old hatbox, which was itself a still more sentimental discovery. This led to a search by a friend in the British Museum, where even the lowliest printed matter is preserved. Other old articles found there were photographed, and finally reached me in white lettering on black paper, looking as if they were in mourning for themselves. That boy could have dressed in them and wept again.

I have, alas, never been in the British Museum (except long ago to dine with Sidney Colvin), though I took my first lodgings in Bloomsbury to be near it. I was told, rightly or wrongly, that I must have two householders to guarantee my respectability, and though my landlady was willing to be one, it was not at the time 'convenient' to the solitary to find another. This difficulty and,

curiously enough, John Morley, were responsible
between them for driving me for ever from certain
heavy intentions.

My emotional discovery, as I have said, was
less that first bundle of pages than the receptacle
that contained them. It was an old leather hat-
box, which was second-hand when it came into
my possession, and before that had gone through
many years of Scottish funerals. To me it was
forwarded soon after I got my first silk hat, my
lum hat as we used to call them, and it was with
this hat that I made my assault on London. Had
it failed me I suppose I should have had to go
back and be a clerk. How it conducted me
through the fray and why I call it the Greenwood
Hat will soon be obvious to the patient reader.
When I re-discovered the hat-box the hat was no
longer in it, nor do I know what ultimately became of it, but I shall tell in my last pages of the
great event in which we two parted with mutual
good-will. This, if properly done, should be as
exciting as the end of a novel.

Out of respect for the hat-box I re-read the
articles to see 'how time with every time is knit,'
or to catch up on Mr. Anon and guess whether
if he and I were now to meet in the street I should
be more displeased with him or he with me. I
must admit that he has it in appearance, judged

by the sketch of him which forms the frontispiece to this volume. It was made in an inspired hour by the celebrated artist, T. L. Gilmour, at that time secretary to Lord Rosebery, in 1886 or 1887 at our lodgings in Grenville Street, hard by Brunswick Square. This is my favourite portrait of Anon, and it is sad to think that T. L. G., the master-hand, so far as I know never made another; he possibly there and then destroyed his tools in a noble self-consciousness that with the first effort he had reached his pinnacle. One regrets, however, that he has omitted the Hat.

Having decided to put this sheaf together in memory of Mr. Anon I may be asked why I have chosen to represent his output by this score or so out of the many hundred contributions he made to the Press in his brief existence. One reason is that most of them have gone beyond easy recall; another is that now that I have tinkered at them extensively, sometimes changing their names, and edited them, these are not, I assure you, the worst ones. They are also more personal to myself; indeed sometimes as autobiographical as the notes I add to them, and thus vaguely they make a story. However inadequate I am to the task of writing a memoir of any one, there may be said to be some excuse for my writing about Anon, for I knew him in the long ago as no one else knew him; we were so close to each other that in this record you will never find him having occasion, to tighten his belt for instance, without my still feeling a similar sinking in the same part of my person. We dwelt inside each other. I once thought of calling the book in a sub-title 'Memories and Fancies,' the fancies (in larger type) being the old articles, and the memories my comments on them. I abandoned the idea, not being always certain, despite the best intentions, where the memories became fancies and the fancies memories. That word, sub-title, is itself a memory to me. Anon began to use sub-titles (now removed) as soon as he discovered that they were worth another sixpence; and long afterwards I learned that Greenwood, our beloved editor, had understood from the first what the hungry Scot was up to and never let on.

In one marked way I must fail completely as a biographer, for I can offer no letters, which, of course, are the staple of such a work as this ought to be. Anon seems unfortunately never to have fallen so low as to preserve private letters for publication. In these circumstances I crave forgiveness for offering articles in lieu of them. They do, I think, often become a little biographical if instead of saying, 'Being somewhat lonely, Anon was glad to get the following letter,' I am conceived as saying, 'Being somewhat hungry, Anon sat down to write the following article.'

He has been called by the misunderstanding a whimsical fellow, and it may be that he fell to being that, but such was never his intention before he graduated at Edinburgh University nor for some time afterwards. Locked up within him was a worthy craving to be the heaviest writer of his time. You have heard how the British Museum slammed their doors on that, but he did not altogether surrender hope until (with a letter of introduction) he met with John Morley. I had the honour of Morley's friendship in later years, but Anon only met him on that dreadful occasion. What sort of things did he propose to write? Morley who was then an editor asked, and Anon gave him a choice of three, *The History of Universities*, *A Life of William Cobbett*, and *The Early British Satirists, with Some Account of their Influence on the Period and the Manner in which they Illustrate History*. I have in my possession still Anon's notes about these and still weightier projected works; but Morley, who was all for brightness, decided that the young man was too grave a character to make a living out of literature, and urged him to try first for a competency in his rugged native land.

Anon (though this was not as yet his name)

had begun to send articles to London to Greenwood of the 'St. James's Gazette,' after a year's
leader-writing on a Nottingham paper. Most of
them came back, but a few were used, and on
one of the rejected the glorious man had scribbled,
'But I liked that Scotch thing—any more of
those?' It was Anon's first paper on the Auld
Lichts, and the terrific date of its appearance was
November 17, 1884. In dispatching that article
he thought he had exhausted the subject, but in
no time thereafter he sent off 'An Auld Licht
Funeral' (accepted), which led promptly to 'An
Auld Licht Courtship' (accepted), and henceforth
I tell you he was frequently at his loom weaving
Auld Lichts. There are none of these papers
here, as like a series of smoking ones and others
they afterwards became parts of books. All of
Anon's articles were unsigned during the two
years of writing with which this small volume is
to deal; but that was well for him, as otherwise
it would have been more difficult (as now) to
obtain an entry. Greenwood, always famous for
liking to give the young a chance, enjoyed, when
an anonymous article in his paper was ascribed to
some swell, being able to reply, 'No, it was by
Bob or Bill or Thomas Anon.'

I was not as yet, however, as I have said, one
of his Anons, though an ardent candidate. After

he had passed a dozen or so of my offerings I wrote to him from Dumfries, where I was then staying with my brother, of my ambition to hie London-wards and my Scottish confidence that I could live on a pound a week. I did not ask for a place on the paper, and indeed, except for that year at Nottingham, I have been a 'free-lance' all my days. I did, however, promise to abide by his decision. It came promptly, telling me to stay where I was till he saw more of my work. So, to put it bluntly, I set off for London next week, on the night of March 28, 1885.

Strange that I cannot remember what the weather was like that night, I who have made so much use of weather in the first pages of less moving tales. Let us survey our hero as he sits awake in a corner of his railway compartment, well aware that the end of it must be to perch, or to let go, like a bat in the darkness behind the shutter. He has a suspicious eye, poor gomeril, for any fellow-traveller who is civil to him. He is gauche and inarticulate, and as thin as a pencil but not so long (and is going to be thinner). Expression, an uncomfortable blank. Wears thick boots (with nails in them), which he will polish specially for social functions. Carries on his person a silver watch bought for him by his father from a pedlar on fourteenth birthday (that was a day). Carries it still, No. 57841. Has no complete dress-suit in his wooden box, but can look every inch as if attired in such when backed against a wall. Manners, full of nails like his boots. Ladies have decided that he is of no account, and he already knows this and has private anguish thereanent. Hates sentiment as a slave may hate his master. Only asset, except a pecuniary one, is a certain grimness about not being beaten. Pecuniary asset, twelve pounds in a secret pocket which he sometimes presses, as if it were his heart. He can hear, as you may, the hopes and fears that are thumping inside him. That bigger thump means that the train has reached St. Pancras station.

Now we come to our first article, which is about the rooks of Dumfriesshire.

CHAPTER II

"My morning walk is under the Rookery when
the green buds are still in danger of being
strangled in a scarf of rime. The air is not then
alive with cawing busybodies; but I have ceased
to be such a coxcomb as to think that I have
caught them sleeping. I meet them in straggling
parties in the open, where they are poking their
beaks among grassy tufts by the ditch in quest
of dew-worms. In the proverb about leaving our
couch betimes, the Rook is the early bird and
the dew-worms are the laggards. In these frosty
mornings he has often a careworn bill. As a
delicacy he prefers the succulent grub to the
sweetest seed that was ever sown, but when a
hard crust of earth forms between him and his
breakfast he becomes a vegetarian. Starvation
drives him from field to street, where, with his

* The method followed throughout the book is to begin each
chapter with an old article, and to follow it with a commentary of
recent date.

10

heart very near that bill, he flutters into a granary and is off with a whole seed before the deftest throw can get him. He clutters over his thefts, admitting his guilt, and looks so wicked in his suit of rusty black that he is generally esteemed the most impudent of thieves. Yet one sparrow popping from street to street may be of lower morals than a whole Rookery. Except among themselves, theft is a rarity with Rooks and is looked down on in the home circle, while sparrows enjoy nothing so much as police surveillance.

The Rook becomes composed after breakfast and takes a rosier view of life. Circling round the tree-tops and cawing as he flies, he reminds one of the gentleman in the 'Canterbury Tales' who was certainly busy but nevertheless seemed busier than he was. I know no other bird familiar to the inhabitants of towns with so complete an indifference to the affairs of men. Rooks like the proximity of houses because they know man is helpful in supplying food; but as for his toiling and spinning, which is an endless amusement to the sparrow, it concerns them not. From the highest tree-tops they see him crawling along the shabby earth, but unless he should happen to have a gun they take no notice of the plodding back-bent clown. The object of the one we are looking at is to get that beautiful twig out of his neighbour's nest. Certainly it is a fine twig; but watchful is the eye of its owner. To sit solemnly blinking at another's possession is suspicious, so Mr. Rook and his wife go off on a caw together. Nothing could look more innocent; but still that twig is in their eye. Their circles become smaller, and they are a little hurt to find the proud owner still sitting on his jewel of a twig. Between friends there should be no suspicions. The couple separate. Mrs. Rook drops down on her neighbour to gossip and innocently kicks the twig overboard. It flutters toward earth, when the other conspirator pounces on it, under the impression that it is the property of the wind, and carries it off to his own nest. This kind of thing is to be seen any day, and when you have watched the comedy so far I advise you to go away. For now begins a deafening din. 'Hullo, what is up now?' caw a hundred Rooks, rushing to the despoiled nest; and as they have a keen sense of justice, woe to the guilty bird who has no defence.

'Caw-caw' is mistaken for the call of the Rooks. They spend the greater part of their lives trying to say this but never quite manage it. Some of them think they do, but the others undeceive them. It is probably known among the older ones that there never yet was a Rook who could master the 'c' sound. It is more like 'Aw-aw' or perhaps 'Awr-awr,' an imitation of the first man who approached a tree with a saw. The other morning I watched two lofty Rooks rehearsing by themselves. They were on the same branch. 'Look here,' said one, 'I flatter myself I have got it at last; pay particular attention to the "c" sound, "Aw-aw."' 'Can't say I catch it,' said the other, 'you should bring it out more like this, "Awr-awr."' Then the first Rook hopped nearer the other and, rising on his tiptoes, exclaimed, 'By no means—observe,' and then croaked 'Aw-aw' triumphantly down the other's throat. They were still at it, but less raucously, when I left.

I should like to feel sure that I shall never encounter a second Rook suffering from a severe cold. My walk the other morning was by the river; and there I fell in with a male bird who should have been in bed with a stocking round his throat. A hoarse Rook makes a whole Rookery rage, for they are sensitive to mockery, especially from one of themselves; and this one had evidently been ostracized. He now grubbed for himself among the garbage of the river within sound of his old home. It is not unusual for Rooks to gad about the banks of rivers in the hope of lighting upon stranded worms or insects;

and this poor creature had perhaps got his feet wet in the puddles. He was a forlorn bird, apparently without hope of regaining either his voice or standing. 'Rawk-rawk' he wheezed forth, and shook his wings in abasement. I expect, however, to see him again consoling himself with grubs; he is the misunderstood invalid with a fine appetite.

Just now we have an opportunity of watching the houses of the Rooks being built or undergoing repairs. A cruel blast of wind made sad havoc of the Rookery last spring, blowing the floors out of half of the nests and carrying the sticks to every corner of the country. The green sward beneath was dismal to contemplate next morning, though some farmers who will not be on terms with a good friend bore the sight with equanimity. The ground beneath the trees showed the white and yellow of eggs, like snowdrops and primroses, as if boys had passed by; ever and again bits of nests, giving way after a brave resistance, flopped to the ground. The Rooks were in a sad way and hovered about the trees commiserating with each other and filling the wood with their wailing. This year they are as gay as ever. If they remember last year's wreckage, it has only been to make them better builders. It is amusing to watch these birds struggling with twigs twice the length

of themselves. I have seen them turned topsy-
turvy by the unwonted weight and shape; but
dire must be their predicament before they will
leave go their hold. The stick has to be steered
with caution. In the first place, one does well
to guard it from envious eyes until it is woven
into the nest, when you can brag about it as much
as you like, and indeed do; and then again it
has a heartbreaking trick of sticking among the
branches that bar the way to the nest. In our
Rookery you may almost any day see some one
of these builders squatting on a branch with a
love of a twig in his mouth, puzzling out the
safest way to the nest. If the stick is very heavy
he flits with it from tree to tree, backing between
close branches when needs be, or trying the
effect of a strategic movement sideways. At
other times he mounts high and reaches his
destination with a swoop. One does not require
to climb the giddy heights to know that there are
no eggs as yet; for the female is at present as
noisy as the male, and with the eggs will come
silence. Then the expectant father goes out
alone to look for the family bread, and you may
see him feeding his wife on his return.

I write in the evening. Nearly an hour ago
the Rooks sailed homeward through the sky.
They go together and they return together. But

though they are home betimes, they are not always inclined for rest. There is a row in the Rookery to-night. Some impertinent intrusion by an outsider, perhaps, or a dispute about sleeping accommodation."

THAT was an old article in the 'St. James's,' and I now begin my comments, written so many years afterwards. Here is the thrill it gave on that March morning in '85. The baggage of our hero (to whom we are about to give a name) consisted of a powerful square wooden box, which had always accompanied him to the university and taken his uncle and brother before him, though to them it was to Aberdeen. On the inside of its lid there adhere to this day remnants recording their academic distinctions (which were outstanding), but for a doleful reason none of his. Having reached London for the great adventure, he was hauling this box to the left-luggage shed at St. Pancras when his eyes fell upon what was to him the most warming sight in literature. It was the placard of the 'St. James's Gazette' of the previous evening with printed on it in noble letters 'The Rooks begin to Build.' This was

Frederick Greenwood

the title of an article he had sent from Dumfries a few days before. In other dazzling words, having been a minute or so in London, he had made two guineas. This may not seem a great thrill to you, but try it in his circumstances. I remember how he sat on his box and gazed at this glorious news about the rooks. He would have had singular pleasure in drawing the attention of all the other passengers to the placard, even though he had to drag them to it by force.

Forty-five years having elapsed since this event, the romance of my life, I myself can now regard it with comparative calm, but I still hold that it was almost as if Greenwood had met me at the station. Yes, and said, 'I baptize thee James Anon.' Henceforth, let that be his name in these pages except when I forget.

I have no recollection how long Anon sat on his box gazing at that two guineas, but I know the box was finally hauled to its destination, and I hope he stepped into London without too much of an air. I can track him for the rest of the day. London was known to him only, as to Branwell Brontë, by maps, and chiefly by wanderings in a map of Bloomsbury, that district which is so convenient for the British Museum. Before, however, he could seek for a habitation, or even for breakfast, he looked around for more placards

(to make sure, you know), I think without success, but he did procure in Gray's Inn Road a
copy of the paper itself in which he read his
article more often than you will do. In that same
delightful thoroughfare (as he always afterwards
considered it) he breakfasted triumphantly, on
what I forget, but we may be sure it was chiefly
on rooks.

The remainder of his programme for the first
day was carried out as arranged at home, coat
buttoned against burglars. Looking for lodgings
he was more than once alarmed to find himself
by mistake in a boarding-house, the outer door
closed, and a majestic black silk dress marching
upon him down the stair. Having escaped these
dangers, he found a resting-place for a brief
period in Guilford Street, where on the table
he at once set out his weapons, consisting mainly
of a desk of the size and methods of a concertina.
He then sallied back into the friendly Gray's Inn
Road and bought the Hat. He also bought a
penny bottle of ink to heave at the metropolis,
and began the heaving before noon. I don't
think his head ever went swimming unless for
those moments when he sat on his box at St.
Pancras. He knew very well that the campaign
was to be a hard one, though not that he should
have fourteen articles returned before there was

a No. 2. The Hat, of course, was bought for the subjection of Greenwood. He understood that without a silk hat he could not advance upon a lordly editor, and from first to last it was used entirely for this purpose every few weeks. It never fitted him (he does not know his size in hats to this day), it was not so much worn as poised on his head, and if, in his walk to or from the St. James's office near Bouverie Street, he suddenly stopped, it as suddenly fell off. He had, however, a religious faith in it, and there is a legend in Fleet Street that he wrote what proved to be No. 2 in his lodgings with the Hat balanced on his head, in the hope that it might change his luck.

By this time he had gone across from swagger Guilford Street (where he was too haughty on the surface to tell the lady that a dinner every day was Brobdingnagian) to little Grenville Street, from which he might for many months thereafter have been seen emerging to dine quite agreeably on four provocative halfpenny buns from a paper bag. Though this was his dinner it must not be thought that he ever went hungry to bed. There was jam and other delicacies from home, and abundance of bread and cheese and tea, and baked potatoes from the oven in the street, with, on gala days, something exquisite from a tin, one of those luscious tins that thought they could defy his knife. He was in that Grenville Street house (which is now splendiferous beyond recognition) off and on for years, sometimes in its finest apartments (all according to the state of his finances), but at first he had a room not much larger than a piano case; it was merely the end of a passage, and was only able to call itself a room because it had a door. It looked on to a blank wall, two or three yards away, with a dank tree between him and the wall. When he stood on the window ledge, as he sometimes did for company, he could count the leaves on the tree. It is there still. As I say, he had always sufficiency of food for a Scot, but he had his shivering fits and he did hanker, you know, for Nos. 2 and 3 to come along. He wished too that he knew some other Anons.

CHAPTER III

" No one who has thought the matter over a little
can escape the conclusion that there are a number
of our fellow-creatures for whom something should
be Done. It may be otherwise, yet I cannot think
that we should be justified in Removing them
against their wish. It would seem, then, that the
time has come for forming a mission Society to
reason with them, to convince them, to strengthen
them in a wise and blest determination to Go.
Further than this, a sub-committee might be
appointed for seeing that the Necessary Arrange-
ments are carried out; and everything should be
gone through decently and quietly. They should
be encouraged to Do it themselves; but where
Assistance appeared absolutely necessary, the
Executive Committee should not see their way to
refuse it.

One thing, however, is certain: if the project
is to be successfully carried out, only men of

known probity can be enrolled on the Society's books. Except in extreme cases, or when the Society is practically unanimous, persuasion should never take the form of force; and, above all, we must start warily. With this object I would suggest that we begin with 'lion comiques.' There no harm could be done, even though the machinery did work badly at first. Not to be too sanguine, we might expect that only one in five would be amenable to reason. As an experiment, what would follow would still be interesting. Friends might have to be talked over; but once convince the principal, and his relatives would surely see that it were better so.

This brings me back to the constitution of the Society. No one would be eligible for election who did not have the welfare of his country at heart, and three black balls would exclude. In certain cases the Committee of Management would have the power to choose persons for Departure without the formality of a ballot; but these would be strictly confined to persons who had already come under the consideration of the Executive Committee and were prepared to meet the Society half-way. As members of the body they would be familiar with this mode of procedure, and, having chosen their own time (within certain limits), could Retire in whatever way they preferred. There would be no fixed entrance-fee or subscription, but the Society would be supported by voluntary contributions. Two books would be kept in the hall of the Society's rooms —one for the use of members, the other for the names and addresses of persons whom in the opinion of not less than two members, it might be well for the Executive Committee to Consider Seriously. To avoid ostentation, one member of committee only would in the first instance pay the person referred to a Business visit; and to facilitate the dispatch of business, London would be divided into districts. There would be branch associations in the provinces, with Birmingham as a suitable centre. Each member of committee would have his own district, but with the privilege of calling in the assistance of one other member should the first visit prove unsatisfactory.

There is one danger that must be guarded against. A member of committee having a grudge against some particular individual or body of individuals may get a name entered on the Society's books to gratify private malice. Such action would, of course, render him liable to immediate expulsion. But it cannot be too much insisted on, that if the Society is to do really useful work such mistakes must be avoided. This more especially at first; and hence the prudence of

beginning with 'lion comiques.' Until the
Society is in good working order we must only
use Material of which we are quite sure. Let it
be enacted, too, that in no case shall the subject
for inquiry be visited by any one of those members
who may have entered his name on the Society's
books. This rule must be absolute. It is plain
that men of parts would frequently come under
the Consideration of the Executive Committee;
and as soon as these had come to understand the
reason of being of the Society, they might be
expected to call at the office and thus take the
Initiative into their own hands. This would be
exceedingly gratifying and cheering to both
parties. Cynics of over thirty years of age might
be placed on the books with a note of interroga-
tion to their names. This would be followed by
an inquiry into their life and circumstances: but
only with great delicacy and caution. They
belong to the large class of semi-fit and semi-
proper persons for Attention who will give the
Society more trouble than either of the two
sections of the community between whom they
are the connecting link. The cynic of over
thirty years of age (it would be wrong to consider
him seriously at an earlier age) might Go with the
greatest advantage to himself and the world
generally; or, on the other hand, a sphere might

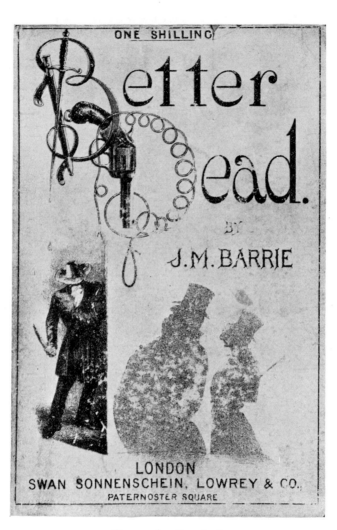

ONE SHILLING

Better
Dead.

BY

J. M. BARRIE

LONDON
SWAN SONNENSCHEIN, LOWREY & CO.,
PATERNOSTER SQUARE

Cover of a first book

still lie open for him. In short, he must be
judged in individual cases, not as a whole; and
to visit him prematurely might be to Lose him
altogether. I look with misgivings on the idea
of taking cases collectively in any instance, and
would even prefer to have comic persons considered one by one. At the same time, should
the Society decide otherwise, I would think him
a poor supporter of a good cause who quarrelled
with the majority of his fellow-members on a
matter of Detail.

To reason kindly but Firmly with the persons
who seem to be lingering by mistake would thus
be the true function of the Society. As fellow-
creatures who feel with them, not as vindictive
enemies, we would approach them with a view
to their Disappearance. I am no apologist for
murder; indeed, it is my deep regard for the
sanctity of life, and a torturing sense of the way
in which it is adulterated, so to speak, by thousands of Spurious Existences, that suggest the
foundation of this Society. The assassin goes to
work in a hostile frame of mind, thirsting for the
gold or blood of his victim; while our Society
is inspired by, and would be conducted on, the
strictest and purest principles of humanity. In
no case would we (as a body) encourage a Re-
moval where less than two-thirds of the Society

voted in its support. The prospectus we propose issuing will contain these words:—'The suicide takes his life because he dare not face his circumstances; while it will be our part to open the eyes of all persons recommended to our consideration to their precise condition. Our representatives or delegates will lay the real state of affairs plainly and succinctly before them, after which it will be for themselves to decide whether they had better Go, or stay on. The Society will supply them with advice, encouragement, and Appliances; but it will assist no one acting under strong emotion, and in all cases six hours must elapse between the final decision and its execution.' Instead of working upon the person's feelings, we shall demand of him the exercise of those higher powers—the intellect and the will. I have thought it wiser to draw up no list of probable Subjects, though these must suggest themselves to any one who has mixed in society. Disappointments there will be assuredly at first; but a sphere of usefulness lies before the Society, if it could get a really good sample for a Beginning."

———————————————

HERE we resume our comments. There was a momentary improvement in the weather (let us call it) during the second half of that April, for not only did 'Better Dead' pierce the gloom, but also 'An Enquiry into Heroines,' and another not at all mysterious about sparrows; indeed Anon stepped into May with several little articles trotting behind him. Then (and so it was to alternate for long stretches) enter three murderers, Rejection, Despair, and the most shuddersome of his callers to a free-lance, the one who knocks not, Silence. In a London fog, though one knows he is in his own street (or so it was in those gas-lit days), he may have to grope for key-holes until at last he finds one in which his key turns. So it often was with Anon trying to open doors with his pen.

Into the night have gone many of his attempts, but heroines he was often to inquire into, and no doubt he turned to sparrows because he had pulled it off with rooks. His sparrows were those that demonstrated vocally of a morning outside his window. Often must they have made previous lodgers wrathful, because they were incapable of coping, but Anon sat at his window and glared at sparrows until at last he made two guineas out of them. They are only worth a friendly mention now as belonging to the days when he made it a stern rule of life, instead of grumbling at misfortunes, to consider whether there might not

be an article in them. As for the rate of pay-
ment, it was princely at a time when I wrote two
stories of twenty thousand words, and received
three guineas for each of them. This also I
gratefully acknowledge, though being done at a
few sittings they left a permanency on my second
finger.

Greenwood was soon suspicious of Anon's
birds, and perhaps let some of them in out of
kindness. He never knew of Anon's dark design,
if the worst came to the worst, which was some
day to go to the Zoo. Here there must be scores
of articles behind little bars and wires. It is a
proof of light dispelling darkness that he never
did go to the Zoo for many years, nor to any other
of the London sights. He certainly soon wrote
about a night he spent among the murderers at
Madame Tussaud's, but where Madame Tussaud's
establishment was he did not know till somewhere
in the 'nineties. For relaxation (it is now horrible
to remember) he liked best to wander the streets
eating his buns. I had a look round for his old
shops the other day, and most of them are gone,
with so much else that once was Bloomsbury.
There still remains one in a little passage between
Southampton Row and Queen's Square, and another in Lamb's Conduit Street, which is now
very battered and has been to let for years, but

'Doig, Baker' still shows vaguely over its shuttered window. Anon, though perhaps the greatest authority of his day on buns, scones and penny tarts (on all of which he has written articles), could be haughty with the purveyors, and would sternly withdraw his custom at the slightest touch of familiarity, as when without waiting for his order they at sight of him began putting four halfpenny buns into a bag.

I note one odd thing about his early articles, that they are mostly written, though anonymously, as the experiences of himself. This is a sure sign that he was still groping for a method. By and by he nearly always assumed a character, writing as a doctor or sandwich-board man, a member of Parliament, a mother, an explorer, a child, a grandsire, a professional beauty, a dog, a cat. He did not know his reason for this, but I can see that it was to escape identifying himself with any views. In the marrow of him was a shrinking from trying to influence any one, and even from expressing an opinion. On an occasion long afterwards when I had to do it I invented a M'Connachie to share the brunt.

This paper, 'Better Dead,' is the original fragment of Anon's first little book, published at the price of a shilling fully two years afterwards at his own expense. He lost about £25 over this transaction. By that time one could have waded in the articles of his that were printed in the 'St. James's,' but why this one should have encouraged Anon to its enlargement I cannot see; however insignificant the others are this one seems to me among the smallest of the catch. Nevertheless from no other book of his had he such a lively rush of blood to the head as when 'Better Dead' was first placed in his hands. For a week or more he carried it in his pocket, he felt for it with his fingers, and slipped into passages to make sure that some sentence was still there.

The cover of the book, which is certainly the best of it, shows the then well-known figures of Sir William Harcourt and Lord Randolph Churchill about to turn a street corner where the well-intentioned hero is waiting for them with an upraised knife. I have been lent a copy for reproduction, as the only 'first edition' I seem to possess of my works is the third volume of 'The Little Minister.' The designer of this cover of 'Better Dead' was William Mitchell, an old school friend of Dumfries days, with whom I used to wait at pit doors in Edinburgh to be haunted by the dire orbs of Irving. The hero is called Andrew Riach, in order to associate him with Sandy Riach, one of the new friends Anon gradually made in London, and among the best of all. Anon read the work to him chapter by chapter, and Riach listened with proud delight to his depredations. I like the book in memory because I see his face at those readings and the smoking-cap in which Anon insisted on his hearing them. Sandy Riach was the only person who led me into crime. He begged me (and I fell), as one uninterested in politics, to let him have the satisfaction of being able to say that he had bribed me into voting for I know not whom with a glass of beer. This, I think, was the only time I was ever in a London pub. I have, however, been wilder than that.

Lord Randolph was not only one of the few people who wrote to the author about 'Better Dead,' but he was also the first. Rivers will run uphill before we forget our first. I hope this book is better than the article, but I shall never know for certain. No author can have more pleasure in revising his works, or even in rewriting them in proof, but once publication has taken place they and I never salute again.

However, we are now far ahead of our date. One thing I should like to know is whether Anon wrote 'Better Dead,' the article, in a gloomy mood because of the rejection of so many of his effusions. If so, it may have been directed against the other Anons who forestalled him in the 'St.

James's,' some of whom I was to know in later years. They were of course people who in his interest would have been 'better dead.' I hope there is nothing in this, however, as one of them, then I think at Oxford, is now the highest Prelate in the land, and has stated that my industry on the 'St. James's' was what made him turn to another calling.

CHAPTER IV

"A SMALL LATH"—CARLYLE AND THE CARLYLES

"Cock-crowing as a disturbance to the sedentary man's peace came up again for hearing; and we agreed as usual that the only way to stop it was to kill the cock. However, an inventor now steps in and says Not at all. Stop the crowing is his plan.

It can be done very easily. All that is required is 'a small lath suspended about eighteen inches above the perch.' A cock cannot crow without stretching his neck, and when he stretches his neck his comb strikes sharply against the lath. Cocks cannot endure having their combs touched; and so this simple contrivance reduces them to silence. Had the invention been known of in Thomas Carlyle's time, the lath in his neighbour's back premises would have been the lever of Archimedes, and it would have rested on a henhouse spar. Alas, ah me.

It was not the crowing itself that turned Carlyle into a dyspeptic, but the awful intervals of silence while he waited. The days were too

short to banish the horrors of the night; an
unseen cock sat on his shoulder as he wrote;
it strutted behind him in his Chelsea walks, and
was never so threatening as when silent. On
such occasions he would have given folios to hear
it crow. It blackened his existence, and when
he had visitors it took their form. Most of the
savage sayings Mr. Froude has chronicled were
really addressed to the cock.

What a different man Carlyle would have been
had his neighbour's henhouse had a small lath.
Instead of hundreds of books about him, there
would have been an autobiography, 'My Sunny
Self, by T. Carlyle.' Mr. Froude would have
been asked to edit it; but, after looking through
the materials placed at his disposal, would have
said that they were hopelessly good-natured. The
genial work would have consisted largely of
extracts from the sage's diaries, private letters,
and reminiscences of friends. We see his cheery
face as he writes:—'June 24, 185–. Had just
sat down to my desk, unwieldy lump of mis-
shapen ash painted mahogany, false faced, yet
inexpressibly dear, when Leigh Hunt's head in
the doorway. Away with musty records. No
more digging for mummies; hand forth, head
forward to welcome heartiest friend of me.
Leigh Hunt, innocent, guileless, scintillating

creature, truly preferring dandelions to guineas.
Ah, we have little growth of that kind in windy
Scotland. He stays to tea, twittering enchant-
ingly. How he draws Jeanie out, and how merrily
their words clash—self rubbing hands and eyeing
the sparks. When Hunt goes Jeanie comes into
my room and tats (mysterious play with wooden
spikes called tatting-needles), while her husband
smokes the pipe of peace; and we agree that
Hunt's great charm is his affection for his species:
best of human qualities; light, bright feather
of a man, yet dagont loveable.' A little further
on, 'December 23, 186–. Jeanie Welsh, Jeanie
Welsh, look upon the man you promised to love,
honour, and obey. Here must I huddle in a
corner far from the writing tools, because the
whole house, no less, is needed for a Children's
Party. And am I truly, then, to crawl on all
fours beneath a hearth-rug to amuse these
youngsters? Ah, well, so shall it be, Jeanie
woman, you grand divert of me.'

Had these been fair samples of the book,
countless newspaper articles would have had to
be written on other subjects. The 'Saturday
Review' would have slated somebody else; the
'Spectator' have preached on other texts; scores
of writers would have been hacked to pieces
who now enjoy a high reputation; thousands

who have got their amusement from the 'Reminiscences' or the 'Letters' would have had to patronize the theatre. Numbers of young men, instead of falling into the sere, would have frequented 'At Homes' and been pierced by maidens. Some would have gone in for racing and made a fortune; others would have gone in for racing and been welshed. Those who ran round to the circulating library in slippers to get the third volume, and caught cold and died, would be flourishing mothers and doting dads.

So much talk was there about whether Mr. Froude had been discreet that in the news-sheets 'Another insult to the British Flag' was printed in small type and never taken seriously. In other circumstances the country would have been roused, and there would have been a war. France would have taken the opportunity to march into Germany; Germany would have bribed Russia by offering to assist her to our Indian Empire. It is probable that our dogs would never have been muzzled; exhibitions at South Kensington might have remained in the egg; half the smokers of Great Britain might have perished of tobacco grown in Herefordshire.

But those things were not to be; no one had thought of the lath."

When in later days circumstances were 'easier,' and my splendid father made his grand visit to London (he could read the Bible with such awful reverence as I have never heard from a pulpit), the first place we sought out together was neither Westminster Abbey nor the Tower, but Carlyle's house in Cheyne Row. In our Scottish home the name that bulked largest next to Burns was Carlyle. It is not surprising, therefore, that before our Anon had been long in Grenville Street, Carlyle was appearing in various guises in the 'St. James's.' I can recall Edinburgh days when I was in full sail in Carlylese, quite the 'sedulous ape,' indeed he was the only writer I ever tried to imitate. I revelled in reading R. L. S. on style, but it depressed me also, and I had a childish notion (which I passed on to Anon) that style is, in a sentence, the way in which you paint your picture. The proper definition is of course far more difficult than that. Nevertheless, Anon inherited a revered approach to Carlyle, and I am surprised to see that in the first of various papers on the great man he dared to be somewhat playful. One would have expected to find him, so to speak, approaching Carlyle in the Hat.

When I was at school in Dumfries I often saw Carlyle in cloak, sombrero and staff, mooning along our country roads, a tortured mind painfully alone even to the eyes of a boy. He was visiting his brother-in-law, Dr. Aitken, retired, and I always took off my cap to him. I daresay I paid this homage fifty times, but never was there any response. Once I seized a babe, who was my niece, and ran with her in my arms to a spot which I saw he was approaching; my object that in future years she should be able to say that she had once touched the great Carlyle. I did bring them within touching distance, but there my courage failed me, and the two passed each other to meet no more. He may have thought me one of the tribe who tried to get a word from him for storage by asking, for instance, if this was the road to Lochmaben, when he would undo them by pointing out the way with his staff and silently wander on.

This is a recollection of many years ago, and I know not whether visitors still come from afar to gaze at his birthplace in Ecclefechan, which is not far from Dumfries. In my boyhood they went in numbers. There was, for instance, an American clergyman who reverently sipped of the polluted water of the burn and carried off a stone from it as a relic in his pocket-handkerchief.

Carlyle's brother James I got to know a little in Ecclefechan and at his son's farm of Priestlands, a shorter man than Thomas, and not near so like him as the son promised to be, but with similar keen eyes, shaggy hair, and rugged lines. My brother was school inspecting at Ecclefechan when I first met James Carlyle in a comparatively talkative mood (for they could all be as taciturn as the great one), and he said to me with a grand burr, 'You make a terrible to-do nowadays about education by what was the case in my young days. One day at the school when I was a nine-year-old my teacher was hearing me say my catechers (catechism), and I said "he believes" instead of "he believeth." He knocked me down and pulled my lugs and banged me on the desks; and I ran out and lay at the foot of a hedge among dockens and nettles for three whole days.' Three whole days seems a long time for a nine-year-old, but they were queer ones, the Carlyles. Grimly attached as they certainly were, they were famed among grim neighbours for the way they 'took each other off' round their ingle-neuk, and in my youth there were still octogenarians able to recall red fires, granite faces, and fierce talk. 'You need not expect us to go out of our way to belaud the Carlyles,' more than one patriarch said, but they had some of the Carlylean humour themselves, and seem often to have accosted Thomas to find out whether he was genial to-day, or ready to flay them. One story told was at the expense of a relative, a tradesman in the little town, notorious for a habit of standing in his doorway thoughtfully scratching his elbows. He propounded a poser one day, 'And what would you say, Mr. Carlyle, is the greatest pleasure in life?' Mr. Carlyle was, as we all know, profoundly learned on the subject, and he replied, 'To scratch the place that's itchy.' He used a better word than itchy, but only Scots would understand.

CHAPTER V

"LOVE ME NEVER OR FOR EVER"—LITERARY VAGRANTS IN HOLYWELL STREET

"'LOVE Me Never or for Ever' (writes 'Disillusioned') was the title of my only published novel, and as the months rolled by I had a craving, surely not altogether venal, to see some one buy it. Any one would have done. It was in three volumes, a form whose drawback, as I shall explain, is that the author cannot see his book bought. It is natural that he should like to be present at this transaction, to watch the customer's eye upon the volumes, to hear him ask the price, to observe his hesitation, to gloat over his inability to put off the purchase till to-morrow, to see him pay his money across the counter; yes, even to follow him to his home on the chance of his reading the first chapter in the streets, to save his life at the crossings, and to walk up and down in front of his house, looking at his pleasant shadow on the blind. This must be a familiar joy to authors in one volume, but it may hardly be done with the three deckers. They are bought only by the libraries, who send round a sort of ennobled wheelbarrow for them.

The best place at which I could hear about my book was not, as it ought to have been, in the newspapers, but at Mudie's. The young men there did not seem to know that I was the author; or perhaps when I asked them (with a shake in my voice) whether they had a novel called 'Love Me Never or for Ever,' they would have said 'Yes,' or even 'Yes indeed,' instead of passing the question from one to the other. I got 'Love Me Never or for Ever' three times out of Mudie's, so that they must have thought I liked it. On the third occasion I asked in as casual a tone as I could assume whether there was a run on it, and was told that this was the fourth time it had been asked for. Two of the other times I had been the subscriber; but the third time—who had got it the third time? I ask that here, but could not summon courage to put the question to the young men at Mudie's. I don't even know whether it was a man or a woman; I think in this case I should prefer a man. What did he think of it? Perhaps he was married, and so there were really two of them. Was he a town or country subscriber? These conjectures however are idle now.

I had nigh ceased to read 'Love Me Never

or for Ever,' when one day I saw it on a shelf
in Holywell Street: one of those shelves outside the window, where you may read as many
books as you like without buying them (by taking
them a few pages at a time on your way home
from the office). It was marked 'By a popular
writer, 924 pp.; the three vols. 1s. 9d.: worth 2s.'
This was not perhaps quite correct; for it is idle
to pretend that I am a popular writer; and 'Love
Me Never' (my pet name for it, as you might
say Peg dear or Bess my love) was certainly
worth more than 2s. Nevertheless this unexpected meeting strangely affected me; for I had
never seen my novel exhibited for sale before.
It had been advertised in the publishers' columns
once; yet I never felt exactly what were the joys
and pangs of fatherhood until I saw that copy.
I was timid of approaching it at first, pretending
to look at the other books, but all the time with
a loving nod for it. Getting nearer and nearer,
I at length had it warm in my hands. I examined
each volume, saw that my name was there (just
as in my own copy), and looked to see that the
first volume had the preface about good wine
needing no bush. Nobody had been tampering
with my work. Then I viewed the effect from
the opposite pavement. The situation was so new
and charming that I could hardly tear myself away.

I was there again next afternoon. When I
arrived a man was looking at volume 2. He was
of a full habit of body, in a bluish-grey tweed
suit, the sleeves of which were so short that I
could see he either did not wear cuffs or from
personal reasons had pushed them out of sight;
the general impression was of marked intelligence. He was in the middle of the second
volume, at the point where Lady Mary makes an
excuse for leaving the two lovers together. Once
I could swear he chuckled to himself; that was
where Lord John bursts into the room and finds
Henry on his knees. That he was interested in
the story there is no doubt whatever in my mind;
he perused it for a quarter of an hour at the
lowest computation ; and before he left he looked
at the end of the last volume to see how it finished.
I have always thought that he would have bought
the book if he could have afforded it. However, the best judges of literature are not always
in affluent circumstances, and I liked to see him
turning in that way to the last page.

It was several days after this before I saw 'Love
Me Never or for Ever' in any one's hands. The
next reader was a young woman, and when I
saw her approach I had a presentiment that she
would pick me up. She was young, of prepos-
sessing appearance, and had blue eyes capable

of melting softness; her dress was a becoming combination in which grey predominated; her hands were small, white and shapely, and her feet were encased in shoes. It was as clear a case of attraction at first sight as I ever saw, for she pushed several other three-volume novels aside with an imperious gesture, and pounced—there is no other word for it—on 'Love Me Never or for Ever.' Unhappily, she could scarcely have reached the meeting in the lane when she struck some other books with her elbow and knocked them over. I saw her glance apprehensively first at the books on the pavement and then at the shop door. Instinctively I knew she was meditating flight. 'Don't be alarmed,' I said, stepping forward to rescue the book; but when I lifted my head it was to see her vanish into the Strand. Perhaps I had been foolish to interfere; but I had no time to weigh the possible consequences.

This was not by any means my only disappointment. I think it was the very next day that I thought the book had been sold. One of the shopmen came out, cast his eye over the three-volume novels, and took away 'Love Me Never or for Ever,' to the chagrin, as I was conscious, of the other novels. I had observed an elderly gentleman enter the shop a few minutes before, and it at once struck me that he must have asked if they had a novel with a certain attractive title. Perhaps he was the father of the lady who got the book at Mudie's, and she had entreated him to buy her a copy. Or he might be her lover, for though no longer young he was well preserved, and had heard her lamenting the accident. I got close to the door to have another look at him. He was quietly dressed, and undoubtedly a man of culture. I was puzzled, however, when he came out. He carried no book in his hand. Had he left word where the volumes were to be sent? or was it possible that he might have them in his pockets? I was scanning his shape, when the shopman reappeared with three volumes in his hands. I recognized 'Love Me Never' at once. He put them back in their old place; but I saw even from a distance that there was a new label on them. I reached the shop the moment his back was turned. The slip of paper read, 'Very exciting, 924 pp., 1s. Worth 1s. 6d.'

This gave me some pain, coming at a time when I was least expecting it. Yet I did not desert this shop. Once I heard two men, evidently persons of importance in the world of affairs, talking about it. In justice to myself I must say that I am not given to eavesdropping. Nevertheless there are exceptional moments

when an author is hardly answerable for his
actions. This was one of these; and when I
saw those two men turning over the three-
volume novels, and heard the words, 'Love Me
Never,' I could not resist listening. It was very
little they said, however. One of them offered
to bet the other a 'drink' that a book with such
a title must be by a woman. The other 'took'
him. Then they turned to the title-page to
decide the point; and as soon as they discovered
that I was a man their interest in 'Love Me Never'
ended; they went off to have their degrading
drink.

Gradually I became very cunning, and I still
believe that if I had been left in charge I could
have got that copy sold. More than once I
drew loiterers into looking through the book,
and one all but bought it; he went back and
forward between it and a second-hand trigonometry, but at last he took the trigonometry.
A lady who roused my hopes turned out to be
the author of 'John Mordaunt's Christmas Box'
(in one vol.), in whose interest she was hanging
about. It was soon after this that I could not
help remarking to the attendant that 'Love Me
Never or for Ever' seemed to be a capital novel.
'Then why don't you buy it?' he snarled; 'I see
you here every day.' This shocked me so much

that I absented myself for a week. When I sauntered by again my novel had disappeared. Had it been sold? I was beginning to upbraid myself for having missed the purchase when I observed volumes 1 and 3 in the 2d.-a-volume box. This was more than I could endure, and I raged through the box for the other volume; but volume 2 had gone. I carried home volumes 1 and 3. Though disheartened, I had on reflection this to cheer me, that some one had bought volume 2.

Of an evening I would muse about what sort of person the purchaser might be, sex, occupation and such like fond trifles, but I had no hope of tracking volume 2. I fell into a gentle vein of melancholy, from which I was roused by tidings of a resident of Shepherd's Bush who had sat on a bus and extolled 'Love Me Never.' My friend who told me this did not know the stranger's name, having merely exchanged talk with him on the bus, but described him as a stoutish man in the late thirties, of ruddy complexion and wearing a worsted waistcoat, in the inside pocket of which (made probably for foreign travel) he carried a volume of 'Love Me Never.' My friend (who is no reader) could not tell me which volume it was, but from the first I had a feeling that it was volume 2. I now travelled

occasionally on Shepherd's Bush buses, but without success. The mystery, however, deepened;
for calling at my publisher's, rather pluckily, I
think, to inquire about sales, I received the
astounding information that one person had
ordered six copies, not indeed of the whole work
but of volume 2. In the circumstances, as they
inaptly expressed it, they had let him have them
at a small price. He was a middle-aged man
of full figure, and his colouring was rubicund.
I was in such a daze that without further ques-
tioning I hurried away, and when I came to I
found myself in Oxford Street watching the tops
of buses proceeding to and from Shepherd's
Bush. Next day I again dropped into that publisher's office, really to inquire about the colour
of the worsted waistcoat, and a chance remark
led to their telling me (quite casually) that they
had his name and address, to which they had
forwarded the parcel. The name was Banks,
and the street Niagara Terrace, No. 17.

It was a pleasant terrace with bow-windows on
the first floor admirably adapted for reading
purposes in the long evenings. As I wandered
up and down the little street with a beating
heart I had no intention of intruding on the
privacy of Mr. Banks, I merely wanted to be
near him. But when what was obviously a

doctor's brougham drew up and what was obviously a doctor stepped into it from No. 17, my blood went a-boil. What had that man been doing in that house? My admirer must be ill, he was perhaps very ill. I had waited for him too long to stand on scruples. I hauled at his bell. If my purpose could have been put into words they would have been, 'You shall not pass away, Banks, until I have heard you praise my book.'

He was quite well, and when I explained that I was the author of 'Love Me Never' he grasped my hand in a way that on an ordinary occasion would have made me wince. 'I am proud to see you at my house,' he cried, and grasped my hand still tighter. Then I knew what I meant when I wrote that my Lady Rosaline loved Sir Harry better and better the more he hurt her. Few authors have been more admired than I am by Mr. Banks. But, ochone, ochone.

You see the reason he cherishes 'Love Me Never' is because one of the characters happens to be called William Banks. He too is William. My William Banks is a very secondary person in the book who makes his first appearance in volume 2, and is dispatched out of it (to Australia) before the beginning of the third. That is why Banks of Shepherd's Bush has no use for volumes

1 and 3. The extra copies were got by him for friends as a piece of swank, and they probably think that volume 2 is the complete work. At No. 17 Niagara Terrace the accident of two people, one in a book, and one out of it, being called William Banks is regarded as the brightest and most bewildering of coincidences.

Friends seek to comfort me by saying I should be thankful that the living William takes the coincidence in this way instead of, as usually happens, bringing me up for libel; but I have not told them everything. For instance, Banks of Shepherd's Bush is giving me cause for some uneasiness. The Banks of my creation is described in volume 2 as being a passionate gardener, as always wearing a white hat, as having an odd trick of shaking hands with himself behind his back, of walking on the kerb instead of on the pavement. The Banks of Shepherd's Bush, in his desire to live up to the honour that has come to him so unworthily, is dropping all his own little personalities and assuming those of my Banks. He shakes hands with himself behind his back as if it were a birth-mark, he may be seen in the streets carefully walking on kerbs and on buses wearing a white hat, he has never hitherto put a spade in the ground, but his leisure hours are now spent in digging and planting.

Even more important changes are pending; for example, my Banks did not love his wife. As I have said, 'Love Me Never or for Ever' is my first and last work of fiction. I consider that such encouragement as I have received has not been sufficient to make me try again."

'LOVE ME NEVER' was one of another kind of paper of which a number went to Greenwood, not always to be returned. Anon knew no authors in those days, but he was already evidently interested in the mysterious creatures, and sufficiently smeared with their characteristics to be able to gauge their feelings. As a rather odd result he had afterwards experiences not dissimilar to those he describes, so that such an article as this becomes autobiographical, if that can be said of what preceded the happenings. When he published 'Better Dead' in book form he went in a modified way through the adventures of the unfortunate creator of William Banks. He too was in the throes of his stillborn (for it was little more), he too asked for it at Mudie's with a palpitating heart, and had the same interest in the few buyers; 'Better Dead'

also reached the 2d.-a-volume box in Holywell
Street, where we may conceive the two outcasts,
it and 'Love Me Never,' exchanging a dreary
time of day. Thus does time bring its revenges.

It was not merely in literary matters that Anon
anticipated his experiences. Many things happened to him in later life of which he had already
written a fairly accurate account. Perhaps this is
quite usual; I merely mention it in case it is not.

I am sure he was far oftener in Holywell Street
than was the author of 'Love Me Never.' There
is a delightful sketch by the late Stacy Aumonier
(one of the best, as Mr. Galsworthy has pointed
out, of all writers of short stories) about a group
of Londoners who fell out disastrously in an
endeavour to locate Wych Street, which had
ceased to be. I wanted to pause in the reading
of that story so that I might join the circle and
give my version. Anon often passed through
Wych Street on his way to and from Holywell
Street, so that his verdict should have convinced
even Mr. Aumonier himself, unless indeed that
author had stumped everybody by asking, 'But
where precisely was Holywell Street.' Any one
can stump me about anything with the word
'precisely,' and I cannot say precisely where
Holywell Street in the Strand was, though I
could take the investigator within a few yards of

it. I remember Mrs. Richmond Ritchie (Miss Thackeray) telling me that after she came from Wimbledon to live in Grosvenor Road she had always to go first to Waterloo Station to find her way about in London. If you wanted me to find Holywell Street 'precisely' for you, I think we should have to, as Anon so often did, set out from Grenville Street, Bloomsbury.

Anon frequented Holywell Street (which I venture to say was slightly west of the present Law Courts) because Denny's corner shop was his public library. It was a shabby, narrow alley, perhaps fifty yards in length, vending many shabby things and smelling chiefly of old books, but that corner shop with its outside display drew him to it as if they smelt of things more succulent. In a true sense they did, for many a guinea Anon made by using those outside shelves for reference. He never, so far as I remember, penetrated inside, but once a month or so, even from the beginning, he would throw prudence to the winds and dine, as it were, at the expense of Denny's. A sausage and mash was fourpence (the steam being thrown in for nothing), and for another twopence you could get what was fascinatingly called a 'repeat.' An affair in more epic form was a chop, which you selected yourself and took home to be cooked.

Though Anon respected this library for the reasons indicated, I feel sure that he had no love for it. Never did he trudge elatedly to Holywell Street because he could gather facts about some subject that entranced him. Facts were never pleasing to him. He acquired them with reluctance and got rid of them with relief. He was never on terms with them until he had stood them on their heads. It was nothing more persuasive than the state of his exchequer that dragged him to that corner shop, and he went through several stages of poverty before he sallied thither, game but gloomy. As long as he could turn out fanciful things, he was now at his happiest. 'Love Me Never' is a specimen, and so were all the papers about smoking; if he had smoked at that time he could not have written those papers with as much glee, one might almost say with as much knowledge. Next to these he liked to press his memory for reminiscences of his past, after which, in order of merit, came the reminiscences of his new friends; they did not provide him with these, he plucked imaginary pasts and presents out of them. If all these stages failed for a time he clenched his teeth and went into politics. He was never a reader of newspapers, and going into politics meant for him saying to a friend, 'Tell me what is going on in politics, and I'll stop you as soon as I think I have got my article.' This sometimes worked well, though the article might be only a little squib, and he exercised to the full his right of 'stopping' them. When even this failed he decided that he must become 'informative,' and marched off to Holywell Street, for he had no works of reference in his lodgings; often he had only one book, Roget's 'Thesaurus.' The corner shop offered no guide with whose help you could search for your abstruse subject, you had to roam for it in the general display. Sometimes Anon found it, and at other times he found some other subject, which might, or might not, do just as well. I hope to spare you any specimens of his informative papers, though re-reading some of them in putting this booklet together I have been astounded at the number of things Anon used to know.

A few years ago I was presented by a kindly firm of publishers with an encyclopaedia in many large volumes, and I dote on it but don't know what to do with it. In the meantime I have hidden it behind a screen.

CHAPTER VI

"THE SMALLEST THEATRE"—THE BOY IN THE
CORNER SEAT—BEHIND THE SCENES

"FOR some months I have been housed in a
small provincial town, the smallest, I am told,
in the kingdom that can boast of a theatre which
is never used as a hall or a corn exchange or an
auction room. It is a pretty little building, quite
complete, but so tiny that you smile to it as to a
child when you go in; and, though it is occasionally visited by good companies, it has rarely
been known to 'pay.' Can London theatre-
goers picture a dress circle from which they could
almost shake hands with a man in the pit or
gallery, and with a leap pop on to the stage? It
is not really of course quite so tiny as that, and
no doubt the sensation of smallness arises partly
from your knowing, more or less, every person
in the house, his occupation, and the number of
his family. You know still better those other old
friends, the scenery, who may be said to receive
you with a wink.

We get more for our money than London
gives; and so much of it is the 'legitimate' that

one hardly believes Shakespeare can spell bankruptcy in the little places. What think you of
four Shakespearian plays in a night, with a 'song
and dance' between the pieces, 'Leah, the Jewish
Maiden' flung in as an extra, and the whole con-
cluding with the side-splitting farce of 'Handy
Andy'? We had such fare one evening, the
performance being for the benefit of a company
in distress, whose manager had stolen away leaving them 'stoney.' The Shakespearian pieces of
the evening were 'the sublime tragedy of Hamlet,'
the 'pastoral comedy of As You Like It,' the
'great historical play of Macbeth,' and 'the poetic
tragedy of Romeo and Juliet.' The versions
played were not those known to the London
theatre-goer nor to the student. In London, I
notice, the players who are in the principal piece
of the evening seldom appear in the opening farce.
At our theatre there are no relays of actors; and
the gentleman who was Prince of Denmark from
seven p.m. till eight, was the melancholy Jaques
and Macbeth a little later in the evening, was
throwing kisses from the foot of a balcony to
Juliet about half-past ten, and had an Irish
brogue as Handy Andy at eleven. Mercutio
was killed only to rush on to the next scene as
some one else; and one man played five different
characters, including two of the witches in

'Macbeth.' He also enveloped his person in a white sheet that did duty as a tablecloth in the banquet scene; and when this ghost gesticulated the sheet began to fall off. Then his arms flapped quickly to his sides, like a windmill when the breeze goes unexpectedly down, and he cautiously 'gathered his cloak more closely around him.' He was to be a soldier in a few minutes, and there was already the gleam of tinsel on his legs. This kind of thing, I presume, is what is meant by the 'all-round training' which actors got in the 'palmy days' of provincial stock companies.

The unrehearsed effects at our pocket-edition of a theatre are more amusing, if less exciting, than those known to the London public. To my simple mind 'organized oppositions' pale as a pleasure before a scene enacted here a short time ago. A travelling company had possession of the boards, and the chief scene in the great domestic drama played by them represented a marriage ceremony. Unfortunately, the manageress of the company and the lessee of the theatre differed as to the point on the stage where the altar should be erected. Decidedly at the back of the stage, argued the lessee, who was proud of his altar and wanted to exhibit it where it would be seen to the best advantage. But the lady was less interested in scenic effects than in the acting, and insisted that it should stand at the side, so as to leave room on the small stage for the players. When she came to the theatre in the evening she found the lessee with his mind made up not to give way. She ordered her stage-manager to see to it that the altar was erected according to her directions. The lessee dared him to place it anywhere but at the back. 'Then,' said the lady, 'I refuse to play.' He said she should never again darken the doors of that Theatre Royal. She replied dreadfully that there were a hundred Theatres Royal but only one Clara Montalbion. The audience began to wonder why the curtain did not rise. Presently the lessee advanced to the foot-lights, and, after a few remarks about the respect he had for his patrons, the pleasant relations that had always subsisted between them, and his admiration for Miss Montalbion, explained the situation behind the scenes. He had also a proposal to make: no other than that the scene about which the dispute had arisen should be set first in the way the lady wished, and then as he preferred it. The audience would say which they liked best, and the piece would be played according to their taste. This was done, and by a large majority the spectators favoured the lady's choice. The lessee, who was greatly excited, then made another speech, bowed

to the wishes of the house, and the play proceeded.
It is by such a scene as this that we feel ourselves
drawn closer to the players: we know all about
their little troubles behind the scenes, and they
know all about ours in front. There is a great
deal of sympathy between them and us, though
we have the reputation of being a cold audience.
This is because in so small a theatre one feels
a self-conscious delicacy in applauding. The
eyes of the whole house are on you the moment
you are seen bringing your hands together; you
know that your friends are remarking to each
other that Foster the linen-draper admires the
girl who plays chambermaid, or that he was
tickled at the pun about see-saws and sea-sauce.
Then the chambermaid, in acknowledgment of
the applause, bows to you in such a marked
manner that you go red in your proud face and
your neighbours whisper that you are unaccom-
panied by Mrs. Brown.

A public that takes its Shakespeare four plays
a night, with an 'entire change of programme'
for next evening, must not be too particular
about scenery. In the manipulation of old
canvas, much ingenuity can be displayed, and
doubtless our theatre lessee could 'set' the whole
of 'Hamlet' out of Mr. Irving's view of the
Brocken. Our great scene began life, I think,

as a 'cottage interior'; but it has become so
rubbed and creased that it is willing to oblige
as its own exterior. I have seen it as 'the wall of
Conn the Shaughraun's cottage,' as 'the exterior
of Glamis Castle,' as 'scene in the Tower,' as 'on
the road to Dixie Land,' as a bit of sky, as 'hut
in the woods,' as 'a banquet hall,' as 'lounge in
the castle,' and as 'the pirates' lair.' No wonder
it winks to us when it appears as something else.

A travelling company is not here for many
days (they are never longer than a week) before
every one in the town has met the members in
the street, or gathering flowers on country roads,
or in a boat up the river. It tickles us to see them
smelling the flowers just as your wife might do
or handling the oars as you do yourself. Much
interest is taken in their proceedings, and numbers
of us can tell you not only where they are lodging,
but what accommodation they have and how
much they pay for their rooms and which one
sleeps on the sofa. Captain S. is seen calling on
the manager at his lodgings, and tongues are at
once loosened on his object. The probability
is that he is to give the patronage of the militia
officers to a benefit on Friday night. We had
a good deal of skating in the winter, and one
day some of the members of a company then at
the theatre came to look on. A townsman walked

a few yards to get a chair for one of the ladies;
and by evening it was common talk that the
gallant Mr. Dash had run all the way from the
pond to his home for a chair, and run back with
it on his head through the streets, merely because
the lovely Miss Vavasour had said she felt tired.
On the other hand, the players soon know as
much about us. Their landladies are as ready to
gossip to them as of them; and I always feel when
I go to see a new company that they are on the
lookout for me and know I have a slight squint.
They are not specially interested in us as brothers
and sisters; but they like to know who are theatre-
goers, who need a programme sent as an intima-
tion of their performance, and who are sure to
come without it. Travelling pantomime companies are not long in finding out which of us
have large families.

Even if the entertainment is of the dullest,
the 'front of the house' is still interesting. You
find that your butcher patronizes burlesque, while
your baker likes long slow deaths. You see a
face in the pit that you are sure to remember but
cannot identify; and after a long time you satisfy
yourself that those are the whiskers of your
housemaid's cousin, whom you have observed
occasionally at the kitchen table. You note that
Mr. Roberts generally comes in at half-time, and

draw your own deductions about his means there-from. You shake your head over the way in which Mrs. Jones goes to the theatre without an escort; and when the Jenkins girls come crushing in after the curtain has risen, you call to mind that they are late for everything, even for church. There is always something to interest you in the smallest theatre, even though it may not be the play."

THE theatre I rashly call the smallest in my old article was in Dumfries and was the first I ever entered; so it was the one I liked best. I entered many times in my schooldays, and always tried to get the end seat in the front row of the pit, which was also the front row of the house, as there were no stalls. I sat there to get rid of stage illusion and watch what the performers were doing in the wings. I am like that still, in the sense that though I suppose I don't go to a play nowadays twice in the year I should still be happy and interested looking on at the re-hearsal of anything. Thus I am at least better than James Payn, whom I tried in vain to coax to one of my own rehearsals and who admitted

Mr. Birrell batting—A. E. W. Mason at point—Gilmour coaching

to me such a distaste for the theatre that he said
if he wanted friends to oblige him in some way
he promised to go to a theatre with them as their
reward. Even then he would scoot away if you
forgot for a moment to keep a grip on his sleeve.

I loved that little theatre in Dumfries, for
which Robert Burns once wrote prologues. I
had the good fortune to frequent it in what was
one of its great years (probably 1877). Usually
it was only visited, as the article says, by wandering companies who were thankful to be gone in
a few days, but on it that year descended a famous
actor and manager who kept it open triumphantly
for a whole winter. His name was J. H. Clynes,
and I don't know if he was really the great actor
the boy at the end of the first row thought him.
Anon in after years saw the name of Clynes on
London theatre bills, but never went to a performance lest sadness should come of it. Mr.
Clynes was my first Hamlet, Othello, Macbeth,
and many others, and though he did sometimes
play two and more of them in a night the versions
were not of the kind the article refers to, and the
scenery winked not. I never spoke to him.
Heavens, how could any one have dared! but
I saw Hamlet lift a mug to his lips. I never spoke
to any of them, but I walked behind most of them
as they strolled abroad and I told other boys that

E

I had done so. More than one afterwards played in early pieces of mine. Occasionally Clynes brought 'star' companies to glorify his reign for a few nights, and one of them was J. L. Toole, among whose supporters was George Shelton, who afterwards 'created' the part of Smee in 'Peter Pan,' and since then has hardly been out of the bill.

It was in those schoolboy days that I had an experience not always vouchsafed to greater mortals—I went 'behind the scenes.' This was so tremendous that to write it even now in ordinary ink and as part of a sentence seems an outrage. I lay down my pen and walk my room for a time before I can resume in comparative composure. The play was Mr. Clynes's pantomime of I now know not what, but it was the merriest and wittiest that boy ever saw, and I am sorry that the only line I remember was a play on the manager's name; some one had to say 'I de*clines* the task,' which was always received by the boy in the corner seat with rhapsody, though I daresay he heard as good in London pantomimes afterwards. The occasion of his being allowed to cross into the realms of bliss was the benefit (they were all for benefits in those days) of one of the players, I think the principal boy, who was such a favourite that on the eventful night the house proper could not contain all her admirers. That boy must have had the luck to arrive late, not only his corner seat was gone, but every seat and even standing room, and a score or more would-be patrons left out in the cold. In the astonishing circumstances we were asked if we wouldn't mind coming behind the scenes and making ourselves as small as possible. 'If we wouldn't mind!' I hugged to myself the extraordinary graciousness of the phrase, as well as other events of that Arabian evening, with their culmination, which was when the beautiful lady said to me in passing that her shoe, confound it, was loose as usual. She may have mistaken me for some one else, but it was to me she said it. We never met again. I was speechless and so could not thank her, but I do so now. Is it possible that she meant I could tie those shoe-laces?

Such doings led inevitably to the forming of a dramatic club at school for which I wrote my first play, 'Bandelero the Bandit.' No page of it remains, but though it played for less than half an hour it contained all the most striking scenes that boy had lapped up from his corner seat, and had one character (played by same boy) who was a combination of his favourite characters in fiction, the only two now remembered

being Smike from 'Nicholas Nickleby' and
Wamba from 'Ivanhoe.' I also appeared in
another piece as a young wife, not so much to
show my versatility as because they would not
let me have a more leading part, and in this I
wore a pig-tail cunningly pinned to my hat to
blow away all doubts about my sex. In the
delirium of being cheered when the curtain
revealed us, my husband knocked over the
breakfast-table, and instead of being stage-struck
dumb the wife grandly saved the situation by
putting her arms round his neck and saying
'You clumsy darling.' This must have been
one of the finest instances of presence of mind
ever shown on any stage; but pride in my
histrionic achievements having left me, I am willing
to present it to any other actor who may now
be writing his life and is hard up for reminiscences.
Long afterwards I saw Miss Irene Vanbrugh playing my part and told her that though she was
good she missed some of my womanly touches.

CHAPTER VII

"THE boys (henceforward to be called 'persons')
in the great school of which he is master of a
house naturally call him Old Hyphen because
he has a double-barrelled name. A very good
friend of mine is Old Hyphen; and I am also
partial to my boy who is a member of his establishment. I read Old Hyphen's reports on him
with avidity and sometimes with a chuckle. The
latest report included a confiscated Diary of
Retrousy's, which is my boy's nickname because,
says Retrousy (completely baffling me), of heredi-
tary appearance. I fear however that in fixing
on the term Retrousy the persons imply a certain
cockiness in my boy, which is perhaps divulged
unintentionally in the following gleanings from
the Diary. Hyphen's report, by the way, makes
no comment on this work, except the laconic one,
'The italics in brackets are mine.' This refers,
you will understand, to certain brackets at the
end of Retrousy's entries in the Diary, which

were added after the shameless work fell into
Old Hyphen's hands.

May 26.

I have been reading (Retrousy begins his
journal) an awfully topping Diary called 'Defects
of Schoolmasters,' and the author is a schoolmaster himself, but it isn't like the diaries some
persons keep about 'Get up at 6.30,' a thing they
have to do every day. It is communing with
yourself so as to be a better man and pointing
out the faults of your friends, and this is the
kind of diary I am going to keep. Some persons
know about it and they are egging me on to
make it mostly about Old Hyphen's defects,
and they have offered to listen to readings from
it in my room at a penny each if I pitch it strong
enough. So I have bought an exercise book and
this is the Preface, and I have wrote on the outside for title 'Quadrilateral Triangles' to choke
Old Hyphen off opening it if he comes prowling
into my desk. If he does he will very likely bag
it and send me up to the Lower Beak.

(Retrousy obviously knows my little ways.)

May 27.

I like awfully keeping a diary and there are
tons of things to say. There is something about

me that riles Old Hyphen more than anything.
Most of the persons say it is because of my
argumentative disposition, being considered the
most argumentative junior in the House. When
he has some of us to tea in his drawing-room,
which is the most ghastly misery but there are
hot tea-cakes, the others kick me beneath the
table meaning that they want me to start an
argument with him, and though I know I should
be wise not to do it I cannot refrain. It is sublime to hear the two of us jawing away, and me
doing best, and him trying to be polite because
it is the drawing-room. If it was in Puppy
Hole he would be at me in one bang. Persons
say that such is my effect upon him that as soon
as he sees me his hands itch to be at me. Some
think it is because when I stand up to argue with
him I keep my legs so wide apart and others
think it is because I am rather stout. In the
Diary about the Defects of Schoolmasters the
author says they should 'keep their tempers,
avoiding alike noisy outbursts of rage, a constantly militant attitude, sarcasm and querulousness.' If Old Hyphen would do this he would
be a tip topper, his house being the best in the
school, but his querulousness when you don't
obey him like a shot is hopeless, and he becomes
militant as soon as I try to get a word in. The

author also says 'With common sense and a desire for self-improvement any one can overcome the difficulties of the scholastic profession,' but it would be no good trying to get Old Hyphen to say that he needed self-improvement. I have sometimes wished to shove 'Defects of Schoolmasters' anonymously under his study door but it would be too risky, me being the one he generally picks out first. I offered Crackly Mi. threepence to do it, but he was abashed though stoney.

(O wise Crackly. It gives me, however, the creeps to note that Retrousy is aware of my struggles to be polite to him in the drawingroom.)

May 28.

There was an awfully good go in form to-day. Old Hyphen is a bit of a nut at Scripture, but in a priceless fit of forgetfulness he spoke about 'Joseph sleeping on the pillow of stones.' For half a jiffy I was sorry for him but before I could be any sorrier I piped out 'Don't you think it was Jacob, sir?' I then stood on the defensive, namely ready to get it hot, especially as Cotton giggled, but the old one just looked at me a long time during which I was the centre of admiration, and then he said 'Thank you, Retrousy,' and stung the others for not having noticed his mistake as quickly as I did, and said again, 'Thank you, Retrousy,' in an obliged threatening voice, which gave me the exulting uneasy feeling that he would get me later, but it was worth it.

(*Not at all. I was only thinking what a queer fish he is. I admit he maddens me, but let me put on record before I have another 'go' at him, that, despite his artful ways, he is one of the most truthful boys I have ever had in my house.*)

June 1.

It is absolutely priceless to keep a Diary and I wish I had begun sooner. I now come to the real secret of how to manage boys. It is not in 'Defects of Schoolmasters,' which I have sold for a bob to Silly Billy, but I got it long ago from watching a mother anxious about her progeny, they are Dinkson Ma. and Mi. and I resided with them three days at Christmas and one night their mother did not come down to dinner and so I said had she a rash, and so they told me all and so my politeness changed to admiration. She was going without her dinner because Ma. had killed two chickens with his catapult, and so it came out that she always punished her progenies through herself so as to strike their conscience dumb. Another day Ma. kicked Mi. for bursting a cane-handled bat while digging for worms with it and she let them both go fishing all the same and locked herself in the still-room. A third time when the fruit had disappeared from the sideboard she copied out 100 lines of Virgil Book 2. Her spelling was priceless but I admire her no end and on my return to Old Hyphen's I told him about it in the drawing-room which was the only safe place, and all he said was that he would avenge the poor woman by taking it out of her sons.

(I did, I had them swished for something else.)

June 7.

This was the week of the sports when Pivot prayed for victory in the house fives juniors, and won and nobody thought much about it till he prayed to win the 100 yards and won again, though Anstruther Mi. is heaps better. Then all sorts of persons began to wonder whether it was a good thing to be pi, and two more tried it and won like anything. By afternoon mi'tutor's was the most religious house in the school among the juniors and we carried the quarter and the hammer, both of which Hurlbart's House thought would be a walk-over for them, but they are unre-ligious persons. The queerest thing was when Anstruther challenged Pivot to run the hundred yards again for glory, and they both prayed, and the result was a dead heat. Then some of the big swells in another house got waxy about it and complained to our swells and they had a meeting, being a quorum, and passed a law that the fairest way was for no one to pray for victory, and the next one who did it to be tanned. I didn't pray for victory, being sure of the mile without it for I am never ceasing in my efforts though a slow starter owing to my portly frame, but by a mistake of Old Hyphen's I was swished with the others, and I don't complain, for though nobody knows, I once prayed to be gently sick so as to shirk early chapel.

(*Odd little beggar, he has a great sense of fairness.*)

June 11.

It is rather a swot keeping a Diary but I like the lark of it and it makes me no end reflective, but sometimes it is impossible to think of a way to get round Old Hyphen because he takes things in the wrong spirit. So he took his birthday in the wrong spirit. It was Cotton who found out that yesterday was Old Hyphen's birthday, and so we kept it dark from the seniors in fear of them butting in, and we presented him with an illuminated address done by little Russell who has a gift of painting in three colours though he makes an awful mess of his fingers and is good for nothing else. I was the one chosen to make up the phraseology and his age being fifty I called it his jubilee year and said he ruled by love and not by fear, and we thought he did not need any more self-improvement. I also said we disagreed with the newspaper which called his translations from Catullus a slovenly work, and the way I ended was what took me most time and you would have thought it would have pleased him best, being about in the course of nature he would soon be taken from us but we would keep his memory green. It was Cotton who put the Address on his desk but as soon as Old Hyphen saw that last bit it was at me he glared and I soon got it in the neck. None of us can make out why he did not like that last bit for it was the bit we were surest of.

(*Yes, I believe I completely puzzled the well-intentioned miscreants that day.*)

June 16.

Not many persons could keep up a Diary as long as I am doing it. There has been a heap of bother this week about using cribs, and Old Hyphen is so crusty about it that you dare not tell him things would be all right if he trusted to our honour. When we were doing Horace,

Turkey translated *ignis* 'devouring element,' and down comes Old Hyphen upon him, wanting to know why he didn't say 'fire,' and what he meant by putting *ignis* in the dative. There is not a better intended youth at mi'tutor's than Turkey, and he was willing to say 'fire' if preferred and to put it in whatever case Old Hyphen liked. Old Hyphen pounded away at him saying he could only have got 'devouring element' out of a crib, and it was just to keep the peace that I did not get up and tell that Turkey had got the words from me. In Puppy Hole the long desks have holes in them for ink-bottles, and beneath the holes are ledges, and some persons found out that if you took away your ink-bottle you could put a crib on the ledge and read it through the hole. Instead of trusting to our honour not to do this Old Hyphen finds out about it and if you translate with feelings for beautiful expressions he goes straight and looks at the holes. So yesterday I made a plan to do him and at the same time to charm him. I translated Caesar in the noblest words I could think of and at once he rushes at my ink-hole and peers down it and sees a book on the ledge and shouts out 'I warned you I would make an example of the next one,' and he seizes me by the neck with one hand and draws out the book with the other, and it was not a crib but a copy of his own translation of Catullus I had put there to surprise him, but he took it all in the wrong spirit, not seeing it was a charming thing to do.

(*I made an example of him all right.*)

June 20.

A remarkable phenomenon has been found out about Old Hyphen, and this is that he has a gutta-percha tooth. He makes it himself by softening it near the fire and then he puts it in the place and shapes it and when it hardens it would deceive any people except my form. Once when he sneezed it flew out and hit Cotton in the face and so Cotton preserves it as a relic, and we think Old Hyphen keeps another one in his waistcoat pocket for emergencies, and gutta-percha is now the centre of interest in our community. Some persons say Old Hyphen does not put a thermometer in his mouth to see how bad his cold is but knows how bad it is by the distance the tooth flies out when he sneezes and a shilling has been offered to any person who will ask him if he can lend them a piece of gutta-percha to rub out pencil marks with, but no one has been such an ass as to take it on. Now the wily bird has done us again by going to the dentist,

and Cotton is talking rot saying it cut his eye
open when it hit him, and some persons think
he can get a heap of money out of guarantee
companies if his father is insured for accidents
and think Old Hyphen would have to be a
witness and show the court how he makes them.

(*Oh for a gutta-percha cane.*)

June 26.

'Even as it was in the days of Imperial Caesar
when Rome towered proudly on her seven hills
sending forth his Cohorts to bend the knee of
Cosmos the while yellow Tiber meandered to
hoary Ocean when Athens cradle of Miltiades
smiled through centuries of antiquity smilings
that never were by sea or shore, so in this whirli-
gig will one generation succeed another.'

This is from the prospectus I made about our
junior Parliamentary Debating Society and there
were other bits as good and we had our own
society because the seniors would not let us join
theirs and we had to make Old Hyphen Prime
Minister so as to be able to have a society of our
own, so he never asked me to take office, so I
became leader of the Opposition and it has been
a most awfully ripping time and calling him the
Right Hon. Gentleman and him having to call
me my Rt. Hon. Friend when he was really

wanting to lam into me. The best day was when
I waggled my finger at him same as my father
does in the House of Commons and I said I was
more in sorrow than in anger because the Right
Hon. Gentleman was giving his support to a
national scandal. The thing that made him get
it so hot from me was his moving the adjourn-
ment of the House for Derby Day and I waggled
at him warningly and exclaimed as follows,
'Consider the thousands plunged into the vice
of mourning when they might have had happy
hours if the Rt. Hon. Gentleman had set a
better example' and what made this the nippier
was that Old Hyphen had said things like that
to me and Cotton a month before when he sent
us up to the Lower Beak for taking 6 to 1 on a
dead cert, namely 'Cousin Bella.' Another time
I had to draw him into calling me a jackanapes
so as I could compel him to withdraw but he
just wriggled out of that and so he resigned and
wouldn't let us go to the country.

*(Not a bit of it, Retrousy; you were suffering
from a determination of words to the mouth and
began (unconsciously I think though I cannot
always be quite sure of you) to use Parliamentary
language in 'Puppy Hole.' I asked you one
day if you were ready to construe, and when you
replied 'The answer, sir, is in the negative,' I*

*thought it high time to wind up the Junior
Parliamentary Debating Society.*)

June 30.

It is sickening the way Old Hyphen pokes
about to see what we are up to instead of trusting
to our honour. All the persons think he will
catch me out about the Diary and I only keep
the thing going now to prove I can do him. I
can see he has found out I have a work called
Quadrilateral Triangles, and he has been rum-
maging my desk and found it but the title diddled
him just like I meant it to do, and so I shall catch
it hotter if he bags it in the end. Now he has
found out that it really is my Diary and he comes
back to bag it and behold it is not there. This is
because I suspected his crafty design and so I
changed its hiding place and slipped it down
between the glass of my mirror and the wood
behind the glass. I was just in the nick of time
for by the way my pictures were hanging crooked
I saw he had been examining the backs of them.
You would have thought no honourable preceptor would have thought of the looking-glass
as a likely place but yesterday he was examining
that also and it was a very peculiar thing that
saved me. To get the Diary up out of the
looking-glass is an awful swot because you have

F

to do it with scissors and just as you are getting your fingers on it back it slips, so I shoved it under the carpet meaning to put it back in the mirror when Father Time was favourable, this being the summer half. So when he sneaked in to open the back of the mirror there was nothing there, owing to the Diary being under the carpet and I think I will keep it there now and so Old Hyphen is foiled and I am again his defeater.

(*Found beneath the carpet, July* 1. *Now, my lad, look out for squalls.*)

Here (writes Retrousy's father) the Diary of Quadrilateral Triangles comes to an abrupt end; for, as I have said, the long-suffering Hyphen afterwards passed it on to me. The story is not, however, complete without some extracts from Retrousy's letters to me on the subject.

Letter 1.—I hope you are quite well. There has been a shindy about my diary. I have kept a diary this half to make me improve my mind and it is mostly about mi'tutor, and I called it 'Quadrilateral Triangles' on the cover so as to keep him from fingering it, him being a whale at classics but well known to have come a howler in Maths, but he is always regrettably prowling around to see what his hand can find to do, and doing it with all his might, so he went wandering

beneath my carpet and found my diary and so he
confiscated it and so he looks triumphing at me,
and he little knows how jolly glad I am it is confiscated, me being tired of the wearisome thing
and having to fill up every day, though good fun
at the first go off. I used to read the bits about
him to persons in the Fourth for a penny a go
paid in advance, and they liked it fearfully at
first but only two came to the last reading and
so they are all glad to be done with it same as I
am and so we have scored off our deceived tutor
all along the line and I will now conclude.

Letter 2.—I hope you are quite well. I regret
to announce mi'tutor has done an awful shabby
thing. I told you about my diary being confis-
cate and how glad I was to see the last of it, but
I have not seen the last of it by a long chalk and
so I will explain, so it was this way. I have seen
the last of that diary all right him having doubtless thrown it into the devouring element but he
has made me buy a bigger exercise book, careless
about my having spent the two bob you sent me
so long ago that I have nearly forgotten it and
so he has ordered me to keep the diary going
every day and not less than two hundred words
and to show it to him daily after lock up, and I
can't think of things to say in it with him reading

them and all the persons I used to read it to are jeering at me and saying it serves me right and that it is priceless of him, and so I hate him, because it lets them crow over me, and so I am your sorrowful son and I will now conclude.

Letter 3.—I hope you are quite well. Do you remember saying to me when I came here that mi'tutor was one of the best, and I have not always agreed with your dictum but I think you were jolly well right and he is the cleverest man in the school. Those persons who liked me to read my diary to them and then grinned heartlessly at the way he punished me have now got it in the neck themselves. He found out in the quiet way I have always admired in him who they were and so now he does not make them write hundreds of lines from Caesar when they have been young asses but instead of that he makes them copy out all my old diary which I thought he had burned and so they get sicker and sicker of it and Cotton has had to do it three times already and I am so unpopular among my whilom friends that some of the seniors know my name now and a blue kicked me and mi'tutor caught him at it and made him turn my bit in the diary about cribs into Latin verse, and so I am rather celebrated at last and I will now conclude.

Final letter.—I hope you are quite well. There is a thing you will like to know and so I will tell you, and so it is this, you always asked me what I was going to be when I am man's estate and I have fixed up to be a tutor at this school and to be as much like mi'tutor as I can, and I like him awfully and so I am friends with the persons again because I want them to send their sons to my house when I have one, and so Cotton has promised to send me his two oldest boys and I have promises in writing of one each from Dinkson Mi. and Anstruther and Pivot and Crackly, and I have changed my mind about the baby I didn't like at that new house near ours and I would like you to ask his people if I can have him, and also any others of first class character you know of who would be about the right age when I have a house. Mi'tutor has promised to give me his youngest as the other one will be too old. If I catch any of my pupils calling me Old Retrousy when I have a house I will make them keep a beastly diary and I will now conclude."

OLD HYPHEN and his young friends in an English public school were wild fowl unknown to Anon in the days in which he wrote of them, but they pop up frequently in the 'St. James's' in his first two years, and were a stand-by when the larder was at its lowest. Greenwood could be got with a schoolboy paper when he would not rise to any other fly. In the painter Haydon's memoirs, which is surely one of the half-dozen best in the English tongue, he tells how when all else failed him he could always get a meal or a respite from confinement by painting Napoleon looking at the setting sun or the rising sun, hands behind his back, hands in front, in hat, without hat, holding hat, on foot, on horseback, ascending horse, descending horse, sitting, rising up, about to sit, till the grim time came when there are such entries in his imperishable work as 'Nothing in the house but the last six silver spoons—oh, my God, must paint another Napoleon.' When the public became sated of Napoleons almost as much as he was himself, he turned (having the right to live) to Wellington at Waterloo, Wellington before Waterloo, Wellington after Waterloo, Wellington standing, Wellington sitting, Wellington with spyglass, Wellington without spyglass, Wellington about to raise spyglass, and the Duke was very furious indeed. I suppose a time came when Greenwood hastily returned my schoolboys and my dissertations on tobacco and even my Scottish papers, but for a time they were Anon's leading-strings.

In my early youth I delighted in tales of English school-life, my favourite among the writers of them being Ascott R. Hope. He was the first author to whom I ever wrote a letter, and I remember carefully misspelling many of the words in it because the boys in his books spelt so badly. Ballantyne was another of my gods, and I wrote long afterwards an introduction to one of them in which I stoutly held that men and women should marry young so as to have many children who could read 'The Coral Island.' Marryat is best read for his scenes afloat, but I felt myself ill-treated when his heroes did not get a few chapters at school. Scotland is a land of day schools where you come seldom into social contact with your preceptors, and never, so far as my memory serves, do you try to blow them up with gunpowder. This was the favourite relaxation of Percival Keene and other heroes of the sea-dog, and it was what bewitched me. It costs as much to educate one English boy as scores of Scottish boys, but there was a time when I longed to go, with gunpowder in my box, to an English school. I had a friend of a like mind to whom, after I had gone to school in distant Dumfries, I sent a present of a box of chalks, and he took for granted that they must be apparatus for blowing masters up and put them in the fire and excitedly awaited the explosion.

Anon never seems to have sent any papers on Scottish school life to the 'St. James's,' and I wonder why. Perhaps he did and Greenwood was cold to them. The nearest he came to it was in several articles about his experiences as a Scottish school inspector. I have been re-reading these and find them very informative. Again I wish I knew as much as Anon knew.

He had no particular school in his mind when he wrote these schoolboy papers, probably did not know the names of the English public schools, certainly was ignorant that each of them bristles with a phraseology of its own, which is the derision of the others. In revising them and making many alterations I have dared to identify the school, not by name but by some of their little tricks of words. I got to know these long after Old Hyphen must have retired and Retrousy taken his place, if he ever did so. It is a school I revere. If it is allowable to dedicate a few pages of a book I dedicate 'Old Hyphen' to an English schoolmaster who was one of the finest souls I have known, Hugh Macnaghten.

CHAPTER VIII

"LADIES AT CRICKET"—THE ALLAHAKBARRIE C.C.

"I LAY beneath a cherry tree, the idle spectator of a cricket match between a ladies' school and eleven young women of the neighbourhood. Not long before, I had seen two teams of the softer sex scrimmaging over a football, hardly an edifying spectacle; but here they made a pretty picture, those happy girls, flitting and darting in print and flannel, and the field was vocal with them. The elevens wore at their waists a rose, a red rose for the school girls, for the others a Maréchal Niel; and the victorious side were to leave the field with the rose of the vanquished at their belts.

The captains tossed for first innings in a professional manner: but, owing to a little peculiarity in one of them, who could not toss the coin without throwing up the other arm also, the penny was lost and a postage stamp had to be used; it answered all requirements and was slow in coming down, thus adding to the suspense. Then the Maréchal Niels went to the wickets, of course padless, carrying their bats beneath their arms, while the tail of the 'out' side gathered round the crease to hem in the ball and have a little chat until it came their way. The first representatives of the yellow rose were Miss Rawlins and Miss Thoms, who both played at least as well as a junior boys' team and with fairly straight bats, Miss Thoms getting the first cheer for going out and patting the ground with her bat. The attack was entrusted to Miss Mitchell (swift daisy-cutters) and a tall girl familiarly addressed as 'Georgie' (overhand). The first over was a maiden, but off Georgie's second ball Miss Rawlins scored 1; following it up shortly after-wards by lifting Miss Mitchell heftily to the on for 2. The running between wickets was much faster than that of boys, once the bats-women started, but they lost time in watching the flight of the ball. Miss Thoms gave point a chance off a hard one, which was not taken, and then skied Georgie straight above short mid-on, who shouted 'Mary dear.' I found that 'Mary dear,' at present cover point, was their great catcher, and that wherever the ball was lofted the fieldswomen usually shouted for her. Several singles and a bye followed, and then Miss Mitchell found her way to Miss Rawlins's wicket (one for 11).

The next comer was Miss Philips, who imme-

diately opened out to a tempting one from
Georgie, and put her away to leg for 3. For
this only 2 should have been scored; but long
leg, instead of returning the ball, ran smartly
with it to the stumps and put it personally into
the wicket-keeper's hands. Miss Philips was
now in superb form, and subjected the fielders to
a rare piece of leather-hunting. Having driven
Miss Mitchell for a brace, she cut another ball
quite professionally, for which a couple was
notched, and then running after a wide one, and
overtaking it in the slips, hit it clandestinely for 3.
This brought on Miss Coombes, *vice* Georgie;
but runs still came, and the score stood at 25
after three-quarters of an hour's play. In stealing
a run, however, the batswomen ran into each
other, and before they could extricate themselves
Miss Hibbert had told Miss Coombes what to
do with the ball. (Two for 25.) Miss Epson,
who came in second wicket down, did not seem
at home with Miss Coombes, and, having slipped
her in a fluky manner for 1, had her wickets
spread-eagled. Thirty was brought on soon
afterwards in byes, no long-stop apparently being
securable who would do more than hasten alongside the ball. Miss Hibbert was substituted for
Miss Mitchell, in the hope of getting another
wicket before luncheon; but both batswomen

played carefully, never hitting out except when they felt confident of raising the leather high in the air to some place where Mary dear was not fielding.

Play was resumed at 1.45, when the two not-outs (Miss Thoms, 7, and Mrs. Tetch, 0) faced the bowling of Miss Hibbert and Miss Mitchell. Off the former's third ball Miss Thoms—who was now playing with more confidence—should have scored a pair; but Mrs. Tetch, making a mistake as to her destination, rushed off in the direction of third man and was run out. (Four for 34.) Further disaster befell the 'in' side in the next over, Miss Thoms knocking off the bails with the skirt of her dress three times while turning to see whether Mary was fielding at long leg. She was then given out. Out she went in the jolliest way. They were all like that. Mary caught Miss Curson, and then the only altercation of the match arose, the Maréchal Niel captain coming out to complain that Mary was catching too many, and had no right to catch balls hit in the direction of another fielder. After consultation between the umpires the decision was given in Mary's favour. The two succeeding bats-women failed to score (also because of Mary). (Six, seven and eight for 35.) Mrs. French, the next woman in, fell just as she was getting well set, and retired evidently under the impression that if you fall you are out. Things were now looking black for the Maréchal Niels, but the last wicket gave a deal of trouble, and a change of bowling had to be again resorted to. Miss Leslie drove, lifted, cut and spanked Miss Hibbert hard for 2, 1, 2 and 2, after which the end soon came, owing to Mary. It was charming to see the not-out player who had scored one lifting her cap to the pavilion and the red and yellow roses alike cheering her; but indeed throughout the match the teams played like white men.

The innings of the red rose was opened by Mary dear and Miss Wace, to the bowling of Mrs. French and Miss Leslie. Mary took the first over from Miss Leslie, who has a dangerous delivery, pitching her balls so high that it is extremely difficult to reach them. Mary, however, has a leap that can reach anything, and 10 soon went up. The scoring now became fast and furious, Mary obtaining a complete mastery of the bowling and becoming so excited that she attempted once to catch herself.

With the score at 20, Mrs. Tetch was tried at the pavilion end, but was only allowed to bowl one over, Mary hitting her so hard that it took five fielders to bring the ball back.

At 26 Miss Wace, whose shoe-lace had become undone, hit her wickets while retying it, and the next comer got a blob. With two of the best wickets down for 26, the prospects of the 'in' side were now less bright. Mary continued to smite them; but was at last dismissed by a cup of cocoa brought to her amid applause, or at any rate by the next ball, which fell into the hands of Miss Leslie, who found it there after looking for it on the ground. After a short interval for what was evidently the most delicious conversation, play was resumed. The result seemed a foregone conclusion with the score at 35 for three wickets; but a remarkable change came over the aspect of the game when Miss Curson was put on to bowl. In her first over she almost did the hat trick, her delivery being so swift that even the slips fled. With only four wickets to fall and 8 runs to get to win there was still a possibility of the Maréchal Niels pulling the match out of the fire, and the fielding now became so smart and clean that Miss Mitchell was thrown out by Mary, who had come on as substitute for a fielder. Bets in gloves were offered and taken by the two fieldswomen nearest me. By byes and singles the score rose slowly to 41, when Miss Mousey was cleverly run out, the stumps being knocked down at both ends. Miss Curson had now gone

completely off her form, and Mrs. French was
again tried. At 42 Miss Croall would have been
run out if Mrs. Tetch had not paused to dust
the ball before returning it. This lost the Maréchal Niels the match, for at 5.30 Miss Croall
made the winning hit, a dashing blow into the
deep, which was caught by Mary but not until
the needed 1 had been run.

The gaiety of them was a new delight on
cricket fields. The most successful bowlers were
Miss Curson, who took three wickets for 7 runs,
and Miss Leslie (three for 14). When all is said
and done, however, the match was Mary dear's,
who, I am incredibly informed, is a school-marm
and the mother of two. I was also told that she
cried on the way home because she thought she
was such a rotten catcher. The distribution of the
roses of the fallen among the victors was delight-
fully formal but ended in a gay race to the pavilion.
As for myself, I continued to eat cherries; it
seemed the right thing to do, in thankfulness for
the lingering sun and for merry ladies."

It is sobering to reflect that on the sunny afternoon when Anon wrote of ladies at cricket, the

most elderly Test Match players of to-day were
in their bassinettes. Ladies nowadays, I understand, play in pads, and I almost wish Anon had
put the toppers of old on the heads of his two
teams. It would have enabled us to visualise
them more picturesquely and been another com-
pliment to the Hat.

Cricket had been my joy since I first saw it
played in infancy by valiant performers in my
native parts, and Anon was not long in London
before he found his way to Lord's. The most
charming sight he saw there was at an Eton and
Harrow match. Among the dense crowd moving
slowly round the ground stood a babe, an Etonian
'scug,' more properly attired than any other
mortal may hope to be, but a-weary and asleep.
In this sleep he stood, buffeted this way and that,
but tile, socks, rosette, cane hooked on arm and
all continued to function correctly—the perfect
little gentleman.

In those days you could sit on the sward and
watch the play as at a country match, but now I
am such a swell that I look on from the little
hotel on the left as you go in. We have got to
know each other there, and I call the attendant
I buy the ticket from George. Anon went alone
to Lord's at first and did not dare speak to any
one, but by his second year he was accompanied

by friends, such as Gilmour, already darkly
referred to and to be more fully exposed presently,
and Marriott Watson with whom Anon afterwards wrote a play.   Sometimes the three of
them went for long tramps in Surrey, oftenmost
to lovely Shere, in which village, 'over the
butcher's shop,' Meredith told me he had written
one of his novels.   On these occasions they talked
so much cricket that it began to be felt among
them that they were hidden adepts at the game,
and an ambition came over them to unveil.   This
was strengthened by the elderly appearance of
the Shere team, whom they decided to challenge
after letting them grow one year older.   Anon
was appointed captain (by chicanery it is said
by the survivors), and he thought there would be
no difficulty in getting a stout XI. together,
literary men being such authorities on the willow.
On the eventful day, however, he found out in
the railway compartment by which they advanced
upon Shere that he had to coach more than one
of his players in the finesse of the game: which
was the side of the bat you hit with, for instance.
In so far as was feasible they also practised in the
train.   Two of the team were African travellers
of renown, Paul du Chaillu of gorilla fame and
the much loved Joseph Thomson of Masailand.
When a name for the team was being discussed,

G

Anon, now grown despondent, asked these two what was the 'African' for 'Heaven help us,' and they gave him 'Allahakbar.' So they decided to call themselves the Allahakbars, afterwards changed with complimentary intention to the Allahakbarries.

The Allahakbarries played a few matches yearly for several summers, that first one being the most ignominious. On the glorious hill-top of Albury where they were overwhelmed that day by Shere, Anon rashly allowed practice bowling, and one of the first balls sent down (by Bernard Partridge) loosened two teeth in the head of the prospective wicket-keeper, who was thus debarred from taking any further part in the game. Anon won the toss, to the indignation of his side, until they learned that this did not necessitate their going in first, and indeed he took the field to teach the Allahakbarries the game, first telling them what to do when the umpire said 'Over.' Unfortunately Shere had a horribly competent left-hander who at once set about smiting the bowling, and as this entailed constant changes in the field besides those ordered by the umpires the less gifted of the Allahakbarries decided that their captain knew no more about the rules than themselves. There were many other painful incidents, among them the conduct of du Chaillu, who stole away every few minutes and had to be pursued and brought back in custody.

It is immaterial now how many runs Shere made, but the score was a goodly one, and Partridge could do nothing to the teeth of any of them. At last, however, they were out, and the once long-looked-for time arrived for the Allahakbarries to go in. There was no longer a thirsty desire on the part of any of the team to open the innings, but in its place a passionate determination that this honour should be the captain's. I forget whether he yielded to the general wish, but at all events he ordered Marriott Watson to be No. 2, because all the time they were in the train, when others trembled, Marriott had kept saying gamely, 'Intellect always tells in the end.' For a lovely moment we thought it was to tell here, for he hit his first ball so hard that the Allahakbarries were at the beginning of a volley of cheers when they saw him coming out, caught at point by the curate. The captain amassed two. One man who partnered him was somewhat pedantic and before taking centre (as they were all instructed to do) signed to Anon that he had a secret to confide. It proved to be 'Should I strike the ball to however small an extent I shall run with considerable velocity.'

He did not have to run. The top scorer (as he tells to this day) was Gilmour, who swears he made five. The total was eleven.

The next time the Allahakbarries played Shere they won because they arrived two men short. They scoured the country in a wagonette, seeking to complete their team, and took with them, despite his protests, an artist whom they found in a field painting cows. They were still more fortunate in finding a soldier sitting with two ladies outside a pub. He agreed to accompany them if they would take the ladies also, and all three were taken. This unknown was the Allahakbarrie who carried the team that day to victory, and the last they saw of him he was sitting outside another pub with another two ladies.

Soon it became clear to Anon that the more distinguished as authors his men were the worse they played. Conan Doyle was the chief exception to this depressing rule, but after all, others did occasionally have their day, as when A. E. W. Mason, fast bowler, 'ran through' the opposing side, though one never knew in advance whether he was more likely to send the bails flying or to hit square leg in the stomach. Augustine Birrell once hit so hard that he smashed the bat of Anon, which had been kindly lent him, and instead of grieving he called out gloriously, 'Fetch me some more bats.' Maurice Hewlett could sometimes look well set just before he came out. E. V. Lucas had (unfortunately) a style. Will Meredith would have excelled in the long field but for his way of shouting 'Boundary' when a fast ball approached him. Owen Seaman knew (or so he said) how to cut. Henry Ford was, even more than Tate, an unlucky bowler. Jerome once made two fours. Charles Whibley threw in unerringly but in the wrong direction. You should have seen Charles Furze as wicket-keeper, but you would have had to be quick about it as Anon had so soon to try some one else. Gilmour could at least continue to prate about his five. The team had no tail, that is to say, they would have done just as well had they begun at the other end. Yet when strengthened in the weaker points of their armour, namely in batting and bowling, by outsiders surreptitiously introduced, they occasionally astounded the tented field, as when by mistake they challenged Esher, a club of renown, and beat them by hundreds; an Allah-akbarrie (whose literary qualifications I cannot remember) notching a century. Anon never would play Esher again, though they begged him to do so almost on bended knee.

Rivalry ran at its noblest when the Allahak-

barries had their bouts with Broadway in Worcestershire, the scene of contests and suppers of
Homeric splendour, at which fair ladies looked
sympathetic as their heroes told of their deeds
of long ago, including Gilmour's five. It was
on such an occasion that Anon presented them
with their Blues while Broadway's rafters rang.
A. F. de Navarro and Turley Smith, both well-
beloved, were the nominal captains of Broadway,
but behind them stood the far more threatening
figure of Worcestershire's loveliest resident,
Madame de Navarro, the famous Mary Ander-
son. Turley cared little which side won, nor
did we, but far otherwise was it with that im-
placable one, who never (such is the glory of
woman) could follow the game, despite deep
study, and always called it 'crickets.' She had
however a powerful way of wandering round the
field with the Allahakbarries' top scorer, who
when he came back would tell Anon sheepishly
that he had promised to play for her in the second
innings.

Anon twice made little books about the 'Broadway Week,' the first consisting of four pages, but
the second was swollen to thirty, just as Wisden
grows and grows. They were privately printed
in tiny editions, and are rareties now, for most of
them have gone for ever with the sound of the

Allahakbarrie bat and ball.   The first proudly
acclaimed its vice-presidents,

> BEAU AUSTIN, ESQ.
> TERENCE MULVANEY, ESQ.
> OLD MEL, ESQ.
> SERGEANT TROY, ESQ.

Of the creators of these officials only one was
himself a cricketer, Mr. Meredith, and by his
request Anon used to send him telegraphic
communications about the state of the game,
as he said he could not wait till morning.   The
second booklet was adorned with sketches, 'Broadway on a Match Day,' by Lindsay M'Arthur, in
which not a dog or chicken shows, all live things
being at the match; 'The Two Captains,' by
Herman Herkomer, in which Madame de Navarro
has just bowled Anon neck and crop; 'An Indis-
pensable Part of their Luggage,' by E. T. Reed
(a crate of ducks);   Henry Ford's idea of 'How
Partridge Sleeps Now' (in pads);   and 'A Dream
of Alfred Parsons by Himself' (in which he gets
his hundred).   There are also photographs, one
of Birrell and Gilmour being compelled to go in
first (at the end of a rope), and another, still more
sinister, of Anon preparing a spot to suit his
bowling.   In the letterpress no member of the
team escapes Anon's censure, and the whole

('Dedicated to our dear enemy, Mary de Navarro') ends with Owen Seaman's 'Ode to Himself on Making the Winning Hit':—

> Bloody the battle, and the sun was hot,
> When on our ranks there fell an awful rot,
> One bearded warrior, playing like a Blue,
> Had made a prehistoric swipe for two,
> When three, his fellows, noted for their pluck,
> Through inadvertence got a paltry duck.
> Upon the war-path, which was far from flat,
> The foemen's champion had secured a hat,
> And one might hear the dropping of a pin
> When you, heroic sailor-soul, walked in.
> Virgin, and chosen for your facial oddity,
> In you your captain found a rare commodity,
> Omitting not what other men omitted,
> You went to make the winning hit and hit it.

Despite the picture of her capturing the Allahakbarrie captain's wicket, let it be put on record that Madame de Navarro herself never wielded the willow. She, however, watched avidly every ball sent down, and it is remembered how, in a certain single-innings match, when Anon said to her that she need watch no more as his side had already passed the Broadway score, she replied hopefully, 'Yes, but you have still several men to go in.' In the photograph of our Rosalind she is not inditing couplets to Orlando, but obviously

The dear enemy of the Allahakbarries

drawing up a score for Anon's discomfiture. In their love for her the Allahakbarries tried to let her side win, but we were so accomplished it could not be done. I take back all my aspersions on the team. I remember now that we always won. The Allahakbarries were invincible.

CHAPTER IX

"THE CAPTAIN OF THE HOUSE"—EXPOSURE
OF ANON

"WHEN Retrousy was nearly fourteen he wrote
to us from school that there was a possibility
('but don't count on it,' he said) of his bringing
the captain of the house home with him for a
fraction of the holidays. We had little conception at the moment of the tremendous import
of this. The captain we only knew by report
as the 'person' who lifted leg-balls over the
pavilion and was said to have made a joke to
mi'tutor's wife. By and by we understood the
distinction that was to be conferred upon us.
Retrousy instructed his mother to send the
captain a formal invitation addressed 'J. Rawlins,
Esq.' This was done, but in such a way that
Retrousy feared we might lose our illustrious
visitor. 'You shouldn't have asked him for more
than the four days,' Retrousy wrote, 'as he has
promised a heap of persons, and there would
have been no chance of getting him at all if his
people had not been in India.' However, there
came a polite note from the captain, saying that

if he could manage it he would be charmed. In this letter he referred to Retrousy as his young friend. Retrousy wrote shortly afterwards asking his sister Grizel to send him her photograph. 'If you haven't one,' he added, 'what is the colour of your eyes and what is your complexion?' Grizel is eighteen, which is also, I believe, the age of J. Rawlins. We concluded that the captain had been sounding Retrousy about the attractions our home could offer him; but Grizel neither sent her photograph nor any account of her personal appearance. 'It doesn't matter,' Retrousy wrote back; 'I told him you were dark and thickish.' Grizel is fair, and a wand, but her brother had not noticed this.

Up to the very last Retrousy was in an agony lest the captain should disappoint him. 'Don't tell anybody he is coming,' he advised us, 'for of course there is no saying what may happen.' Nevertheless the captain came, and we sent the dog-cart to the station to meet him and Retrousy. On all previous holidays one of us had gone to the station with the cart; but Retrousy wrote asking us not to do so this time. 'Rawlins hates any fuss,' he warned us.

Somewhat to our relief we found the captain more companionable than it would have been reasonable to expect. 'This is Rawlins,' was

Retrousy's simple introduction; but it could not have been done with more pride had he waved a gold rod and our guest been Mr. W. G. Grace himself. One thing that I liked in Rawlins from the first was his consideration for others. When Retrousy's mother and sister embraced our boy on the doorstep, Rawlins pretended not to see. Retrousy frowned, nevertheless, at our false step, and with a red face looked at the captain to see whether he forgave. The captain indicated in the most charming way that he understood and made allowances for the eccentricities of female relatives. With much good taste our boy uttered no open complaint at the time about our breach of manners, and I concluded that he would let it 'slide.' It has so far been a characteristic of him that he can let anything that is disagreeable escape his memory. This time, however, as I subsequently learned, he had only controlled his pain to dump it on his sister. Finding Grizel alone he remarked darkly that this was a nice sort of thing she had done, making a fool of him before the august. Asked coldly what he meant (for Grizel can be freezing on occasion not only to her own brother but to other people's brothers), the injured one inquired hotly if she was going to pretend that she had not kissed him in Rawlins's presence. Grizel

replied that if Rawlins gave him a bad mark for
that (which he didn't) he was a nasty boy; at
which Retrousy echoed 'boy' with a grim laugh,
and said he only hoped she would some day see
the captain when the ground suited his bowling.
Grizel replied contemptuously that the time
would come when both Retrousy and his disagreeable little friend (by the way, it is Rawlins
who is dark and thickish) would be glad to be
kissed; upon which her brother flung out of the
room, protesting that she had no right to bring
such charges.

Though Grizel was thus a little prejudiced
against the captain, he had not been many hours
in the house before we began to feel the honour
that his visit conferred upon us. He was modest
almost to the verge of shyness, though it was the
modesty that is worn by a person who knows he
can afford to be thus attired. While Retrousy
was present Rawlins had no need to boast, as
his worshipper did the boasting for him. When,
however, the captain exerted himself to talk,
Retrousy was content to retire at once into any
obscurity and gaze at him. He would look at
all of us from his seat in the background and
calculate how Rawlins was striking us.

Retrousy's face, as he gazed upon the wonders
of the captain, outreached the rapture of a lover.

He fetched and carried for him, anticipated his wants as if Rawlins had been an invalid, and bore his rebukes meekly. When Rawlins thought that Retrousy was talking too much he had merely to sign to him to shut up, when Retrousy instantly closed.

We noticed one great change in Retrousy. Formerly when he came home for the holidays he had strongly objected to what he called drawing-room calls, but all that was changed. Now he went from house to house showing the captain off. 'This is Rawlins,' remained his favourite form of introduction. He is a boy who can never feel comfortable in a drawing-room, and so the visits were generally of short duration. They had to go because they were due at another house in a quarter of an hour; or he had promised to let Jemmy Clinker see Rawlins (Jemmy is our local cobbler and also sends down curly ones). When a lady engaged the captain in conversation Retrousy did not scruple to lead him away in five minutes; and if they were asked to come again, he said they couldn't promise. There was a memorable entertainment the captain could give with a poker which Retrousy wanted him to present everywhere. It consisted in lying flat on the floor and then raising yourself in an extraordinary way by means of the poker. I believe it is a very difficult feat; and the only time I ever saw our guest prevailed upon to perform it he looked too apoplectic for such a swell. Usually he would not do it, apparently because he was not certain whether it was a dignified proceeding. He found difficulty, nevertheless, in resisting the temptation, and it was the great glory of Retrousy to see him yield to it. From certain noises heard in Retrousy's bedroom it is believed that he is practising the feat himself.

Retrousy, you must be told, is an affectionate boy, and almost demonstrative with Grizel if no one is looking. She is also so devoted to him that she has promised never again to call him 'Pup,' which nickname of childhood would he thinks for ever shame him in Upper Fourth. He was consequently very anxious to know what the captain thought of us all, and brought us our testimonials as proudly as if they were medals awarded for saving life at sea. It is gratifying to me to know that I am the kind of governor Rawlins would have liked himself had he required one. Retrousy's mother, however, is the captain's favourite. She pretended to take the young man's preference as a joke when her son informed her of it; but I am sure she felt elated. If Rawlins had objected to us, it would have put Retrousy in a very awkward position. Grizel

began by asking our visitor if he came down for
late dinner; but has since dropped her hauteur
with him, and to Retrousy's bewilderment the
captain has been seen tying her shoe-laces, and
servilely collecting any articles she dropped on
the floor, which reminds me, by the way, that she
never used to drop things before J. Rawlins
arrived.

On the night before his departure J. Rawlins
addressed me privately thus with dreadful humility
and cunning: 'I was thinking, sir—well I don't
know but I just thought—it doesn't matter—it
came into my head you see—I haven't any sisters
—how would you do it—I don't mean you—but
if you knew a girl—well, a girl you knew—not
that it matters—and you wanted to tell her—the
girl I mean—that in your opinion—if it was you
—I don't mean a relative—I mean I don't mean
my relative—but if you wanted to say it fright-
fully—and you knew her young brother—I mean
if you wanted to tell her you thought her an
awfully pretty girl—and you were staying in the
house, you see—and of course it being the last
night—how would you do it?'

I won't tell what my reply was—not being the
girl, you see—I mean only being her father, you
know; and on the whole we were perhaps glad
when Rawlins left, for it was somewhat trying

to live up to him. Retrousy's mother, too, has discovered that her boy has become round-shouldered, and it is believed that this is the result of a habit acquired when in Rawlins's company of leaning forward to catch what other people are saying about him. As for Grizel, when Rawlins's name is mentioned, she says, 'Absurd little Pup,' but she smiles and says it leniently. I have written that word with a capital P because the rumour is that as he was leaving he asked her to call him by his Christian name (Jack) and she said she could not, but if he liked she would call him Pup, to which (it is painful to relate) he replied 'Thanks awfully.' In commendation of Grizel it should be mentioned that she has not told Retrousy about this, but we feel that she is holding it over his head."

Is this all ludicrously out of date? Harry and Miss Dolly, to whom I have foolishly shown the article, say that Anon was possibly a darling but certainly a chunk. They good-naturedly refuse to believe that the boys and girls of the past were ever so ludicrously different from themselves, and have reconstructed the scene for me as it really was.

H

Harry cannot believe that at any period in the world's history a father could have written with such abysmal ignorance of his young.

Miss Dolly is not so sure of this, for she has a comic duck of a papa herself. She thinks the father might have written it in good faith, and that Anon's dunderheadedness lay in not seeing what inevitably followed; namely, Retrousy and J. Rawlins and Grizel got hold of the MS. and Grizel read it aloud to the other two amidst much merry laughter at the dear old man's conception of them.

One thing Harry could not understand was why Retrousy thought it necessary to ask his mother to invite J. Rawlins to the house.

This did not puzzle Miss Dolly in the least. She has read old fogey books of the period, and it was always done in them. It was just an example of the hypocrisy and want of frankness of the Victorians. Anon had been quite right in having that letter written; where he showed a thick wit was in not seeing that it was merely a blind. The visit had of course all been arranged before the parents ever heard of J. Rawlins. Neither Retrousy nor J. Rawlins arranged it. It was all taken in hand by Grizel, who sent word to her young brother asking him to be a sport and bring an older sport with him for the holidays, as home life was become unendurable owing to their parents having gone dotty on the question of the upbringing of the young. J. Rawlins on being shown this communication decided that Grizel must be a promising kid, and the date of visit was then fixed, the remark of J. Rawlins being told to Grizel, who blushed with gratification.

Harry thought it must have been a dull house of an evening, for old Retrousy seemed to be the kind of cove who sent the young ones off to bed before he retired himself.

Of course he was and did, Miss Dolly explained, but after he was asleep (and Anon also) the three slipped down again in disarray (or perhaps only two of them), and had a you-know-what time. Miss Dolly could not guess what they poured out, for —— —— (these represent lovely swears) it was before the days of cocktails, but she was magnanimously sure that Grizel was a scream, and in better days would have been a famous mixer.

Harry wondered what J. Rawlins was up to when he told the old boy of his feelings for Grizel.

Miss Dolly supplied the information. It was really Grizel who made up that halting speech for him, so that J. Rawlins and she (she was behind the door) could afterwards roar with laughter at Pops for swallowing it whole.

There was much more of it till they went off to the tennis court. I can't tell you how thankful I am that they are unaware of my connection with the dense Anon. (Now, now, Mr. Editor, enough of this, you know very well that you are all on the side of the woman of to-day. Yes, indeed I am, though not of every sample of her.)

CHAPTER X

"I HAVE just returned from the Elysian Fields,
where I went to inquire of Shakespeare whether
he really was the author of his plays. He was
not there, nor could I hear that he had ever
been elected, but I got in touch with a few of his
contemporaries. According to some of them
there never was any such person. The majority,
however, including Kit Marlowe and the actors
Cowley and Burbage, remember one Will Shakespeare, who used to sell unauthorized bills of the
play outside the Globe Theatre. Though illit-
erate, Shakespeare seems to have been a smart
young blade, and to have made a more or less
respectable livelihood in the purlieus of the
theatre. He was a native of Stratford-atte-Bow.

What are called the Shakespearian plays were
not, it appears, written by any one man; but the
Baconians are right to this extent, that Bacon
had a share in them. He was at the head of a
firm for their manufacture, and, though he wrote
nothing himself (even the 'Novum Organum'

117

was written by Tom Nash in association with his friend Gabriel Harvey), he superintended the productions; and it was in a room rented by him in the Saba, a tavern in Gracious Street, that the collaborators met. If the dramatists themselves are to be trusted, and their dress when I saw them hardly justifies this, their arrangement with Bacon was that they should have no risk; they were paid (or as Peele put it 'B. promised to pay us') at the rate of sixpence a folio, and there, so far as they were concerned, the bargain ended.

According to some answers to a circular I distributed among them, the real authorship of the plays was withheld because Bacon wanted by and by (if all went well with them on the first nights) to claim them as his own. This, however, is evidently a mistake. A document kindly shown to me by Walter Raleigh, who was one of the firm, proves what most of them stress in their answers, that it was by their own express wish that the real writers remained anonymous. The little paper referred to (which is now in my possession) is the agreement between Raleigh and Bacon; and in it the Chancellor undertakes to keep Raleigh's connection with the firm hidden so long as Raleigh does him the same service. 'That we should have taken these precautions,'

Raleigh explained, 'is not surprising. I know
not in what estimation, if any, the plays are held
to-day; but of course at sixpence a folio we
could only dash them off in our spare time, and
as most of us had some reputation to lose, we
naturally shunned going down to posterity as the
authors of "Macheath," "Queen Leer," and the
various other plays in which I had a hand.'

In the same connection Greene stated: 'I
must say that I was annoyed as well as surprised
to receive your circular. To your question, Am
I Shakespeare? I answer emphatically, No. Apparently it has leaked out (Did you have it from
Cutting Ball or Mistress Islam?) that I had some
share in the collaboration; and, as usual, the
critics are more anxious to damn a man by
dwelling on his pot-boilers than by calling attention to his more serious efforts. I do not deny
that I touched up some things for the firm—(I
particularly remember one about a melancholy
prince who sold his father to a merchant in
Venice for a pound); but every one connected
with literature surely knows that it is a poorly
paid profession, and that we cannot always write
as we should wish. It was Kempe who introduced me to Bacon in Seacoal Lane, and at that
time I was so stoney that I could not afford to
reject his offer of sixpence a folio. After the

lapse of so many years it does seem hard that this hack-work should be thrown in my teeth.'

Ned Alleyn explained that his share in the plays was confined to practical suggestions as to 'situations' and the like. 'The fact is,' he told me, 'that we should have produced better pieces had we thought the public would stand them. As an actor-manager the success or failure of any one of the plays affected me much more than my collaborators, and this, more than the sixpence a folio, was what induced me to lend a hand. The S. plays were not meant for cold analysis in the study. They were written for the stage, and should be judged solely on their acting merits. I was always strongly averse to their being printed in book form, and so, I remember, was Bacon.'

One of the questions in the circular was, If Shakespeare did not write the plays, how does it happen that his name is attached to them? It seems to have come about rather oddly though Spenser's explanation carries conviction. According to him, when the first play of the series was completed a difficulty arose, the firm wanting to produce it without any author's name. Alleyn, however, set his face against this. The public, he maintained, disliked anonymous writing. As none of the various authors would put his name to the piece, fancy names were suggested. 'Shak-spear' gave most satisfaction, not that it was considered a specially good name, but because of the way at which it was arrived. The collabor-ators were Spenser, Harvey, Alleyn, Kempe, Sly, Peele, Elliman, Atlow, and Raleigh, and the word 'Shakspear' is obtained by arranging the initial letters of these names in the above order. It may be mentioned, as clearing up a disputed point, that the reason why this playwright's name is spelt in so many ways is that occasionally a new man joined the firm or an old member left it. Thus when Greene took Kempe's place the word was spelt Shagspear.

Up to this time only one or two of the dramat-ists knew of the existence of the young man who sold the playbills outside the theatre. All, how-ever, knew him by sight, and Alleyn in par-ticular disliked him. Nevertheless, when the next difficulty arose, namely, who should be the 'middleman' between the firm and the theatre, it was Alleyn who recommended Shakespeare. 'In this,' Gabriel Harvey said to me, 'Alleyn showed some shrewdness. Shakespeare had taken a good deal of money out of Alleyn's pocket by selling bills outside, and Ned was quick to see that this would end if S. became a paid servant of the theatre. The youth was originally engaged simply as a messenger; but when we learned his name, it struck us that we could blind the public still more by pretending that he was the actual author. At first the young man demurred; but Bacon made him a little present (a pair of breeches, not much worn), and he ultimately consented.'

Peele, as already hinted, speaks somewhat bitterly of Bacon's 'promising' to pay at the rate of sixpence a folio. In another part of his communication he says outright that he could never get more than fourpence. As Bacon has taken no notice of the circular, it would probably be unfair to accept all that Peele says of him. In justice to Bacon, also, it should be mentioned that Peele was too fond of practical jokes. Sly assures me that Peele wrote the greater part of 'Henry VIII.,' and that in the original manuscript (it had to be revised) puns were introduced about Wolsey's being the son of a pork-butcher. Bacon suspected that these were jocular references to his own name, and he did not like them. 'Bacon,' said Sly, 'was the touchiest man I ever knew; and it was specially distasteful to him (as indeed to myself) to have to acknowledge S.'s bow in the street. I have nothing to say against S., but he was one of the commoner fellows who played Shuffle Board at the Mermaid.'

My last question was to this effect: If Shake-

speare did not write the plays, how could he have
made sufficient money to retire and live comfortably in Warwickshire? There are various
explanations, but the most interesting is Kempe's,
who says that it was really Lady Bacon who wrote
all the plays, but fearing that her social position
might suffer if this was divulged she paid W. S.
substantial sums for fathering them."

A FEW papers of airy persiflage such as this were
all that Anon ever published about Shakespeare
and his contemporaries, but, as I think I have
already said, they were not all I wrote and still
less all I planned. Marlowe and Peele and Greene
and Gabrielissime Harvey and Tom Nash and
all the others, how I dwelt with them in the Edinburgh University Library and edited them with
voluminous notes of import, the while with the
other hand I reached out for John Skelton, Dun-
bar, Marvell, Mapes, Donne, Prynne. Masson
is said, before he finished his monumental biography, to have known what happened on every
day of Milton's life (though I have always
suspected that he was doubtful about one Wed-
nesday), and if I did not precisely meditate a row

of monuments on a smaller scale, I think that so far as the Shakespearians were concerned I could have drawn a nice little map before ever I saw London of where they lived and wrote and quarrelled and drank and mostly miserably died. They were the only people I searched for on my arrival, and I found some of them ; but I could not have cared enough about them (I sorrowfully admit), else the book would have been written by now. I am not in a hilarious mood when I say this, but it is humorous to remember the one matter in which those labours helped me. When for a start in life I answered an advertisement for a leader-writer in a provincial newspaper, I was asked to send specimens of my leaders, and I, who had never written (nor read) a leader, sent instead a treatise on King Lear. I was appointed; so it was Shakespeare who got me on to the Press.

CHAPTER XI

"THE SADDEST WORD"—DARK PASSAGES IN
ANON'S HISTORY

"I WAS in the Scotch express on my way to
London, and I think it was at Carlisle that five
of them boarded my compartment, all husband-
high. When their packages had been disposed
of and they were comfortably settled in their
seats they turned their eyes on me and gave their
verdict in the deaf-and-dumb alphabet, which
unfortunately I understand. It spelt out the
words 'Quite harmless,' and they then disre-
garded me for the rest of the journey. They
talked openly of the most intimate things as if
I were far away in the guard's van. It is a treat-
ment I am used to, but never perhaps have I
been so blotted out, I who know that with
another face I could be quite harmful.

They were bound, as their conversation showed,
for a wedding where at least two of them were to
be bridesmaids, and had almost as many topics
as chocolates, but the one over which they
lingered most lovingly was the Saddest Word.
A tall poetical-looking girl thought that the

saddest word was Nevermore. She was the loveliest of my scorners, her cheeks of the most delicate carmine and her eyes were like lakes. The fingers with which she had spelt out my doom betokened grace and breeding, while her voice, capable of the most varied modulations, now soft and tender, now deep and mellow, and again clear and bell-like, was of the timbre to stir a man who was not harmless to his innermost soul. Nevermore. The word in her opinion sounded like the wail of a broken heart. It was a judge passing sentence of death. Nevermore. That was what the relentless waves said as they dashed against the sullen rocks, and the seagulls eddying round the cliffs took up the shrill response. What she specially liked about Nevermore was its cruelty. It was as cruel as the grave. Was it not the grave itself, the grave of human hopes and aspiration? It recalled the past only to make the future more bitter. The loved ones, or the loved one of the past, where were they, where was he? Far away across the seas; we should meet him Nevermore. The dances we have had. Ah, the dances we shall have Nevermore. The smiles that were. The warm clasp of the hand that seemed so trivial, that meant so much. The nights on the river, when the boat glided down, shadow-like. The day when first they met and all seemed merry as a marriage bell. All, all are gone. Nevermore. The river glides on; but when shall they see it together again, they and the pale moon? Still the conservatory stands; but is it the conservatory of the days of yore? Ah, Nevermore, Nevermore. She could not look upon a raven now without fancying it croaking forth that doleful solemn word. 'Quoth the raven, Nevermore,' was the saddest line in English poetry.

Nevermore did not seem so inexpressibly mournful as simply 'Never' to a second girl, who was undoubtedly the fairest in the compartment and was sitting on my newspaper. It is no disparagement to the others to say that she shone among them like the moon among stars. Yet were the sun a more fitting emblem, for she seemed a ray of sunshine rather than a being of flesh and blood. She was of a small form of the most enchanting roundness, and her noble head stood on a neck white as the untrodden snow. Her golden hair (or coal-black hair, for at times I got a little confused) escaped from its single band of ribbon, and fell in rich profusion over her shapely shoulders, caressing her delicate shell-like ears, and ever and anon lightly kissing the red pouting lips that men with some harm in them would have gladly done deeds of derring-do to win. Her melting eyes seemed ever on the point of glistening with a tear; and as she spoke falteringly, dreamily, she slowly picked a bun to pieces to get at the currants. Never was sadder than Nevermore because it did not even imply the pleasures of memory. Nevermore meant that though you might now be old and grey there had been moments of happiness to which you could look fondly back. They were gone, but they had been. No such solace could be got from Never. The lover's glance, the hand-pressure, the moments in which one lives a lifetime; it was sad indeed to think that they would be no more, but sadder to think that they had never been. Nevermore was a sentence for the future, Never for the past and the future too. Saddest of all, Never meant that you knew what you had missed, what you must go on missing to the end. The most terrible line in English poetry was not 'Quoth the raven, Nevermore,' but,

Never—for ever ; for ever—Never.

The bells tolled it when the grave was filling, and the aged hills sent back the mournful words. The time to appreciate their significance was in autumn in the woods when all the twigs were bare and the naked trees shivered in the cold.

Wandering through the dead and rustling leaves
(or eating buns in a train), she loved to murmur,
'Never, for ever; for ever, Never.'

The others might be pretty; but the third
speaker was a queen among her sex, majestic,
stately, superb. Her eyes were black as death,
their lashes of the same hue. Eyes wonderful,
fatal not only to others, but to herself. Two
dark arches marked the low brow, and the
creamy skin had the blush that is at once the
painter's admiration and his despair; in tint it
looked like a magnolia petal laid on a rose-leaf.
Her white firm hands were plump and dimpled,
with lissom fingers and cameo nails that might
dig deep on provocation into the kind of man
who was worth while, namely, any man except a
harmless one. She spoke with a seductive voice
that vibrated like sweet music through the compartment. To her, sadder far than any word
was the tragic story told in the phrase It Might
Have Been. Nevermore dealt with the inevitable.
However bitter Never might be, not yours was
the blame. Fate said that what was would be
Nevermore; you had no voice in the matter.
With It Might Have Been all was different.
It implies fault on your part; and what so
bitter in this vale of tears as the consciousness
that you suffer for your own error, your own

I

blindness? It is sackcloth and ashes now, and It Might Have Been bridal garments. It Might Have Been. With these words you are back again at the honeysuckled gate of your youth. Ah, how well you remember it, with its broken spars and the catch that clicked. He came. He was impatient, perhaps; but you, you were coy, and you parted to meet no more. That was the turning-point of your life. You did not realize it then. You know it now. And how easily It Might Have Been. Or it was at the yeomanry ball, and you sat on the stairs with Another. You longed to be with Him, for you had read aright from his eyes the tale he longed to tell; but though your hand would have thrilled to his touch you were mad and you sat on the stairs with Another. Mad, mad. And so he turned on his heel and left you, and the light went out of your life. It Might Have Been.

There is an attraction in some faces beyond all mere physical charm. A girl who thought there was most sadness in the simple words A Faded Flower had an ethereal look that the others lacked. A harmful man would perhaps have admired the others more, but he would have chosen the seat beside her. What was it about her that gave her this subtle fascination? At times you would have said (if you had been sufficiently harmful to be worth listening to) that she was absolutely plain, and yet her face haunted you like a painting by the old Masters. Was it that there was a history in that face, that she was one who had already lived and suffered? She regretted that they had not bought chocolate cakes instead of drops, and it was because A Faded Flower was pathetic rather than tragic that she liked it best. A flower was the emblem of happiness; for it was short-lived. It was here to-day and gone to-morrow. Yet not gone; for the withered stem remained in your hand. The flower was the loved one's gift far more than glittering jewels, for love was a thing that could not be bought, and a flower cost nothing more than a broken heart. If one could write the history of all the faded flowers that have ever been preserved, it would be a history of the heart since the days of Eve.

The fifth girl was such a one as it is the glory of English homes to grow. There is only one description of her: she was an English girl. Of a blooming complexion and elastic step, hers was the beauty of rosy health. She had been obviously a good daughter, and you could not look at her without feeling that she would make a good wife if you were sufficiently harmful to attract her. No other girl is to be mentioned in the same breath with such a one. She thought there was something strangely sad in the words She Never Told Her Love. Think of the unutterable grief of seeing him day by day as the years roll on, and knowing that he thinks she is without a heart. Ah, fate is sometimes hard. He will never know that her love for him is even as his for her.

This girl, who had more buns than any two of the others, specially infuriated me, and it was while she was still prating, as they had all been doing, of the kind of bounder she preferred (for that is what it amounted to) that I began ostentatiously to converse with myself in the deaf-and-dumb alphabet. Having thus got their scared attention at last, I joined briefly in their discussion. 'Ladies,' I said in deaf-and-dumb, 'the saddest words a broken-hearted young man can have applied to him on his journey to London to seek his fortune is that he is "quite harmless."' I then bowed (if the Scotch can bow) and withdrew harmlessly to another compartment."

Did Anon ever hear ladies discussing him for the briefest moment in a train or anywhere else?

Alas, his trouble was that ladies did not discuss him.

Let us at present pointedly ignore the fair ones of that compartment and concentrate with kindly interest on the mean male figure in the corner. I remember (I should think I do) that it was his habit to get into corners. In time the jades put this down to a shrinking modesty, but that was a mistake; it was all owing to a profound dejection about his want of allure. They were right, those ladies in the train; 'quite harmless' summed him up, however he may have writhed (or be writhing still). I am not speaking about how he appealed to man, but about how he did not appeal to woman. Observe him in that compartment. Though insignificant he is not ugly. To be ugly, if you are sufficiently ugly, is said to attract the wayward creatures. The rubber that blotted Anon out is called (and it deserved a big word) Individuality. Anon has read and thought (with resentment) a great deal about individuality, one of the delicious characteristics of which is expressed in the words said to be so common on the lips of woman, 'The sort of man, my dear, who wherever he may be, is always the centre of it; when you enter a room, without seeing him you know he is there, when he goes he leaves a blank.' You don't need to be handsome to be this sort of man, but the handsome ones can, in classic language, do it on their heads, and at any rate it is the handsome kind that our poor Anon wants to be. If you could dig deep enough into him you would find first his Rothschildian ambition, which is to earn a pound a day; beneath that is a desire to reach some little niche in literature; but in the marrow you find him vainly weltering to be a favourite of the ladies. All the other cravings he would toss aside for that; he is only striving hard for numbers one and two, because he knows with an everlasting sinking that number three can never be for him. If they would dislike him or fear him it would be something, but it is crushing to be just harmless.

We continue to survey him in the train. You who don't know him conclude that he is sitting on one side of the compartment instead of the other side because, say, he likes to face the engine. Not a bit of it. I who remember know that he is sitting there in order not to face the mirror. On one side of railway compartments (as you know so well) there is often a tiny narrow mirror, and our Mr. Anon prefers to sit with his back to it. In after years he always pursued this policy, not merely in trains. I have heard people say (or it has been repeated to me) that at such and such a dinner-party he was comparatively bright, while at such another one he had been drearier than ever. They did not know, no one could know without penetrating his sorrowful heart, that in the first case that dreadful mirror over the mantel-shelf was behind him and in the second case in front. He had his most unhappy experiences when there were mirrors north, south, east, and west as in restaurants. I have no recollection of a mirror in his lodgings, but I presume that if there was one he turned its face to the wall.

He heard every other male talked of by lenient ladies (and how lenient they can be about the wrong men) as having some redeeming feature; he was a good listener, or he had a way with him, or his face lit up when he smiled. Anon was a good listener, but could not look as if he were listening, so he might as well have worn Herbert Spencer's ear-flaps. He certainly never had a way with him. (Nobody knows exactly what this is, but if you have it you have reached harbour.) He did, however, once (though the tragic fool was un-aware of it) have a simply irresistible smile. He never even saw it nor any of its effects, but I believe I could bring forward witnesses of it to this day (and have a good mind to do so). The tale is a deplorable one. In early days the school

I attended at Dumfries was a 'mixed' one, whereat the girls, little witting that they were destroying me, once took a plebiscite about which boy had the sweetest smile. It reached my dazed ears that I had come out on top, and in the ensuing exaltation my smile left me for ever. So far as is known I have never smiled since. If ever in those first years in London Anon in privacy twisted his face before a looking-glass, you know what he was trying to bring back.

If those thoughtless girls of my school days had left to me my one asset, Anon's future would probably have been very different. Never would he have become such a monster of a labourer. Sufficient for him to have devastated female society. Once (if you will excuse my drivelling) he did seem about to achieve a solitary triumph. A beautiful lady did actually agree to accompany him to a daring luncheon for two at a riverside hotel. (How those memories cling.) He was to hire a carriage (such were the dimensions of the affair), and call for her in it at her address; he did hire it, but when he was half-way to the hotel he found that he was alone; in some imbecile reflections on mundane matters he had forgotten her. He drove back hurriedly, but was hopeless enough to tell her why he was so late; and I suppose that luncheon for two is waiting for them still. What is such a man to do with himself except plod on writing weary novels and plays? That I can now see clearly is why I at last took to those callings. Perhaps it is why all novelists and playwrights take to them.

CHAPTER XII

"THE BLUE AND WHITE ROOM"—CONTINUATION
OF THE DARK PASSAGES

"THERE is a saying that hopelessly good-natured people look at life through coloured spectacles. Leonora, whom I am visiting, would not thank you for looking at this room through them unless she chose the colour. They might not harmonize with the room, which is blue and white; and she would resent the intrusion of any spectacles that were not blue. The first night I spent in this room I noticed that the blind was tied up in such a way that it could not flutter down. Snow had fallen all day, and when I put my head on the pillow the cold back garden shone like a white ghost through the window. I did not like it, and I said so next morning. Leonora, who has been married for quite two months, explained that the effect of the snow was so good against the blue of the room. I think this was my first flash into what her spare room had become to her. I have been writing here, and a few minutes ago I caught myself at my old trick of jerking my pen behind me; result, the wall shows ink spots. Had they been blue I could have faced them, but woe is me

138

to spill black in Leonora's blue and white room.
Nevertheless this does give me a subject to write
about. I dip in Leonora's blue bottle, and resume
in chastened spirit.

Leonora's husband is a doctor, and he has a
sense of humour. Many a time have I said
things that have made him throw back his head.
But when I mentioned the blue and white room
he uncrossed his legs nervously. We were down
stairs in the surgery; but he glanced hurriedly
at the door and put down his mortar. I caught
him looking covertly at me; and after an uncanny
silence he said, 'The blue and white room,' as if
he had said much more. When he had gone into
the anteroom where he dispenses bottles between
six and seven o'clock, I sat on ruminating. Truths
gradually revealed themselves to me, and I saw
that his reserve was manly. There are subjects
which are best not discussed, even between friends;
and since then I have not mentioned the blue and
white room to him. Yet when we bade each other
good-night that evening it was with an unusual
grip of the hands; we understood each other.
My grip meant that, though he was a married
man who had consequently brought it on himself,
I sympathized with him; and his meant that had
he had his way I should not have to sleep in the
blue and white room.

To say that the bedroom is a study in blue and white is not to do it justice. In the furnishing of this room Leonora discloses a genius which we thought she almost lacked in her maiden days. I found this out gradually. The person who occupies the blue and white room never knows all at a glance. He is always finding out something new (in blue or white). The room grows upon him; and with it admiration for Leonora. Take for instance the books. One day the doctor missed from his library a medical treatise; he could find it nowhere. The lady of the house was questioned, and she suggested that he should make use of one of the other treatises instead. This sent him prowling. He went straight to the blue and white room, and returned with the treatise (which is bound in blue). I was induced thereby to make a scrutiny of the book-shelf in my bedroom. All the bindings are blue or white or both. I discovered that the gentle but dogged Leonora had searched the library for volumes suitable for the blue and white bedroom; and the books suitable for a blue and white bedroom are books that are bound in blue and white. They are not a happy family on that shelf. There are two of Black's novels (I am sure she would like to change his name to Blue), a parliamentary handbook, a Thomson and Tait's 'Elements of

Natural Philosophy,' an 'Anatomy,' and several other medical works, a copy of 'Horace,' two time-tables, etc. To-day I notice that a parliamentary blue-book has been added. It was too large for the shelf, so was laid in a provocative attitude on the dressing-table.

Leonora is not one of those second-raters who decorate a room and have done with it. She is always adding something. Yesterday in the surgery I missed a packet of my own envelopes, kept together by a blue paper band. So I sought my bedroom, and there they were on a small table beside an ink-bottle, the one in which I am now dipping. The match-box is hand painted in blue and white, and so are two photograph frames. I have with me a brown dressing-case which vexed her for several days. One day I saw her sewing what looked like a small blue pillow case; and soon afterwards I found my bag inside this garment. My initials had been neatly marked in blue upon a white label. One of Leonora's few failures is the coal-scuttle. It is a tiny wooden one, and she had painted it a delicate blue, with a white handle for the shovel. But the fire did for that delicate blue. So the scuttle has gone, and coals being of an outrageous colour, logs are now brought from the kitchen by a maid who wears a white cap with blue ribbons. I have not mentioned the slippers. They had been specially sewn by Leonora for the blue and white room, so I need not tell their colour. They are not meant for use, but they look very well at the side of the fireplace beneath the white bellows which blow blue smoke from the logs.

Let it not be supposed that there is no education in a blue and white room. When Leonora married she was the only girl in the family who could not or would not sew. Now behold over the mantelshelf the wool-work which I boldly call tapestry in two colours. As for painting, she never knew in her maiden days how to hold the brush; yet who, daringly perched on crazy steps, painted that Mediterranean ceiling? Our Leonora. What made her fit to do this? The call of the blue and white room. When I have made the journey of the room I cease from smiling, I marvel at the concatenation of things, and remembering how economical she has to be in her new home I praise Leonora."

I THINK the story of the Blue and White Room must have been dispatched without re-reading,

for I see no embroidery on it, and Anon certainly
tended to embroider. He might have called it
with gentle pride a real autobiography at last, one
of quite a few old articles in this book wherein
the memoirs are seldom tripped up by fancies.
In studying catalogues of, say, first editions, I
am often lost in admiration of the noble candour
with which the compilers thereof say of a book,
'rebacked,' or 'a few leaves mended,' or 'title-
page defective,' or 'margins slightly stained,' or
'bindings worn,' or 'advertisement at end torn.'
If Mr. Anon was expected to be as truthful as
that in his articles, and to keep saying in brackets
'Here my fancy takes the reins,' or 'memory at
this point slightly defective'; if in short the law
had compelled him to guarantee all his statements,
he would have been constantly a case for the
police.

The Blue and White Room, however, was a
real room, and as far as I can remember he leaves
it as he found it, not a white atom added nor a blue
one omitted. It was the work of art of a sister of
mine, lately married. In the days of the glory of
the Blue and White Room when Anon wrote of
it he may have been sarcastic about its adorn-
ments, and perhaps I was trying to make amends
for this when I afterwards put some of its pretty
furniture into my play of 'Quality Street.' Anon

liked visiting that room during those first years of London, as much as he shuddered over most of his visits elsewhere. Not that there were many of them, but they loomed because the awkward man only knew his way about in lodgings.

I observe that others when they travel are for ever in a worry lest their luggage should go astray. I never had this trouble, as it was always my custom when setting out on those dreadful 'week-end' visits to very nice people to carry in my pockets every belonging that I considered of value. All my money was there and bulky MSS., and probably a score of letters (so that my pockets must have stood out like brackets), and thus, as it were, attired, I heeded not the fate of my portmanteau. Alas, my very first visit to the affluent showed me that it was not to be so easy as that. I awoke next morning to find all my treasures gone. While I slept thinking no evil of the household, some menial had stolen into the room and wafted them away. He returned my garments, neatly folded, but the precious parts of me were gone. Great was my relief when at last I found them, as neat as the clothes, on a table; but I had got my warning, and thereafter before retiring in strange houses I always hid the contents of my pockets in unlikely places, as on the tops of wardrobes, very difficult for the enemy (and for myself) to scale.

The length of those 'week-ends.' Anon never knew whether he was most sorry for himself or for the lady whom he took in to dinner. She was usually kindly and courteous, striving in a way that went to his heart to put him at his ease, coming back to him refreshed by a talk with her other neighbour; but all in vain. On the rare occasions when he could say anything she was so nervously desirous to listen that she never knew what it was he said. He more or less loved her by the time she saw she must give him up. If he met her on the stair after dinner (which so far as I know even now is the most dire moment that can come to two people in a country house) she smiled sweetly though she was shuddering, and he stalked on to his room to shudder also.

CHAPTER XIII

"A RAG OF PAPER"—DREAM OF A POUND A DAY—MISUNDERSTOOD

"FROM my window I have been watching a rag of paper that is trying to circumnavigate our shapeless 'square.' I look down on the meeting place of five dingy streets, and at the opening of each the rag is caught up in a draught that bears it along to the next or tosses it back to the spot from which it came or even plasters it momentarily on the person of a passer-by. If it adopts pedestrian methods, it trips cautiously in little spurts, like some nice old lady crossing the road; feet trample it, kerbs claw at it, walking-sticks stab it, it adheres momentarily to the wheels of vehicles. The dogged little ragamuffin, however, recovers its breath; it may lie for hours shamming, and then is off again. Watching this paper has become the occupation of my convalescence, though I perceive its grand ambition is only to travel once round the square.

Since this vagabond of the streets hove in sight some days ago a change of Government has threatened, and we have had the riotous mobs

in London which no one sees but the Press.
Before it is borne away from Bloomsbury or
reduced to mire, there may be Events. I have
a wager on the subject with my doctor, who still
drops in to comfort the solitary. It is that this
morsel of paper will outlive the Administration.
Should it not, he gets a stethoscope of the newest,
and if I win he presents no bill. He had misgivings lest, since so many paper scraps wing
their way through the streets until they migrate
for the winter, mine might vanish and its place
be taken by another. He does not allow for the
fascination this rag of gallantry has had for me
since I divined its project. I look for it in the
morning when I am wheeled to the window, and
I can tell at once by its appearance what kind
of night it has had. Nay, more: I believe I am
able to decide the trend of the wind since sun-
down, whether there has been much traffic, and
if the fire engine has been out. There is a fire
station to dignify one of our sordid corners, and
if the heavy wheels run over my little one it has
an excusably crushed look, yet not without a slum
touch of bravado. You can conceive it playing
street urchin at the firemen. However, though
I felt certain that I could pick it out of a flock,
the doctor insisted on making sure. The bet
was arranged during the third or fourth day and

recorded on the scrap itself, the doctor having captured it and brought it to my room for our signatures. It proved to be a fragment of newspaper about the size of a lady's handkerchief, in which the words had long run to mush. Once perhaps an item of momentous intelligence, it was now living a vagrant life of its own. It was become so sloppy that pieces adhered to our fingers and we could only initial it in blobs. Then we opened the window and cast it forth as from a cage. The doctor promised by 99 not to remove it by stealth when evening fell, and I vowed by 98·4 to report progress fairly.

I no longer find time so heavy in my legs; my attention is divided between two papers, the one in the streets that I have backed and my daily copy of the 'Times.' Any morning the absence of the one below may tell me that I have lost my bet, the pages of the other that I have won it. I hobble to the window before they can bring the chair, fearing that my rag of paper has predeceased the Government. Obviously neither of them can last much longer. It is remarkable how greatly my interest in politics has increased since I made this wager.

The doctor, I believe, relies chiefly on the scavengers. He thinks that they are sure to pounce first upon the more tattered object,

though they are after both. For my part I do
not see why I should fear scavengers: they come
into the square so seldom, and stay so short a
time. If he knew how much they kept away
he might say I bribe them. I got a fright,
nevertheless, yesterday from a dog. He was one
of the breed that infest the square in half-dozens,
but seldom alone. He appeared from one of the
side streets with my rag in his mouth. Then he
stood still and looked around. I had a sinking.
The impulse seized me to throw open the sash
and hurl a yorker at the miscreant; but I remembered my promise to the doctor. A man
has seldom been more disturbed by a mongrel.
At one of the street corners there is a melancholy
shop to let; six times within the last two years
have fried fish, toys, ha'penny buns, sorrowful
hearts and the like, which had entered on the
adventure of life in that shop, had to depart in
barrows. A skeleton cat is often to be seen
coming up from the area to lounge in the doorway. To that cat I believe I owed it that so far
I had not lost my wager. The faithful animal
stretched itself; in the act of doing so it caught
sight of the dog, and put up its back. The dog,
resenting this demonstration, dropped its mouth-
ful and made for the foe. I saw the cat victorious
and sank back relieved.

There was a greater alarm within an hour. An unshaven idler looking about for work or a pipe-light, espied the paper frisking light-heartedly on the pavement. He picked it up with the obvious intention of lighting it laboriously at a hot potato stove where I have spent some engaging minutes. The gods being kind, a gay young butcher collided with him, and the loafer, a man and a brother after all when tested, evidently at once asked him for a match. The match too was on my side, and to my infinite relief the quaking scrap was restored to freedom. At this the Government lost heart and went out at 11.45 last night. So to-day's 'Times,' though unaware of the importance of its news, tells me this morning that I have won my bet. Financially this is a relief to me, as otherwise I should have been pinched; but my victory is incomplete, for I cannot lead my rag of paper to the stable it deserves; it may never have the pride of knowing that it was once backed as a winner.

We parted for ever to-day at noon. All morning it had lain in one position, yet with an occasional flutter of the lungs, as if, I thought, the discomfiture of St. Stephen's was not dis-pleasing to it; though I should have known that now, and all the days I watched, it had one single thought—not of politics nor of me, but to make

victoriously the circuit of the square. We are
born for different ends, or so we think, we rags,
and it thought it was born for this. It lay there,
neither exhausted nor boastful, I now feel sure,
but studying the winds, aware that rain was
threatening and dissolution near. It had gone
so thin that but for its mud it would have been
transparent. Of a sudden it rose, lifted, the
materialist might say, by an accidental puff of
wind, but as I know by some nobler palpitation,
and under that guidance went sailing round our
square. It just succeeded, not many feet past
the tape, but it did the round and had an exultant
moment to know that it had won before the rain
swept it into the gutter and it went gamely down
the drain. Hats off."

THOUGH Anon after his first year was so near his
pound a day that he could reach it when he stood
on tiptoe, he always remained a free-lance. Every
few weeks, however, his prince of editors let him
call at the 'St. James's' office, and submit a list
of possible subjects. It was then that the Hat
came into play. Whether Greenwood ever
noticed the Hat in those days will now never

be known, but it encouraged Anon, though often in his way. Greenwood heard of it in the end, as you shall learn in our moving last chapter, which I have already decided to call 'Good-bye to the Hat.'

Those visits to the sanctum, which Anon enjoyed greatly (once they were over), were not very profitable, for among various discoveries he was making about himself was this, that he was incapable (except for a wager) of writing about anything that he announced he was to write about. Some imp within him, who loved to take control, immediately coaxed him away from that subject to another. This holds good with me still (but the word should be bad). Friends who wish me to proceed with a new project always hurry from my presence if I begin to tell them of it.

The rows of subjects that Greenwood passed as possibles and were no more heard of, and the rows he put that pen of his through and were promptly posted to him, no Hat could have held them. He never complained on this score, but he was sometimes nervous over articles which meant the reverse of what they seemed to say, a kind of writing that the imp referred to was constantly egging Anon to write. These brought many letters to the harassed editor from puzzled readers. Greenwood liked to get correspondence

as the result of articles, but not letters (mostly
in a feminine hand) that raged. The only editor
Anon ever had who liked that kind of article was
Henley. There was one in the 'St. James's' of
a journalist who had written so many articles
about the Jubilee that when told to write another
he retired to the study and shot himself. This
was accepted in some quarters as news, and a
provincial paper commenting on it called it one
of the saddest affairs connected with the Jubilee.
More severe language was used about another
in which Anon described himself as having been
so pestered by the Waits that he buried them in
Brunswick Square. One of the letters passed on
by Greenwood to the author said of this, 'The
most cold-blooded murder I ever read about, and
the writer shows no contrition.' There were
many such criticisms, and Greenwood maintained
that every outraged reader represented at least a
dozen more.

Mr. Anon, as has been told, when hard pressed
even wrote what are called 'informative' articles.
Many of these were about his doings in distant
climes, his adventures there, and his occupations,
though had he taken time to reflect he must have
known that he had never left his native island.
One audacious series of the kind described his
experiences in India as a civil engineer, when,

among other deeds, he banked the Irrawaddy, with fifteen thousand coolies under his command. I re-read this lately and found it engrossing; my present-day knowledge of India indeed is largely founded on my recollection of such articles. They fascinated Greenwood, who probably wanted to know about India also, and though he was a little scared of the Irrawaddy he took some more about Anon as second in command of a convict settlement on the Andaman Islands. The series ended with a stern indictment of the Government for paying Anon his pension in rupees. Many retired Civil servants wrote to join in this fight for justice, and thanked the anonymous writer warmly. After this Greenwood let him have his head.

A number of Anon's articles, including the 'Rag of Paper,' were written in answer to challenges from friends who wanted to o'erthrow him. In this case they had pointed to a piece of paper in the gutter and defied him to make two guineas out of it. Strictly speaking, it has no right to be here. Ever since I began making this compilation I have been worried by discovering that papers chosen for it have already been incorporated to some extent in books, and this is one of them. I have discarded the others, but decided to retain this, as it was Greenwood's favourite among the soap-bubbles of Anon.

CHAPTER XIV

"EDUCATIONAL NURSERIES"—HOW A CHILD
DROVE ME INTO THE WILDERNESS

"No one (writes a child of six) who knows what
it is to be brought up on alphabetical biscuits
will wonder at my being able to write an article.
Do not think me proud of it. Acutely I feel the
false position in which an educational nursery has
placed me. Here am I, at the age of six years,
so full of learning that yesterday I had a grey
hair. I spend much of my life between historical
wall-papers, and if I look closely at the ball I
am 'playing' with I find it is a globe of the
Hemispheres. Only the other day I was in-
veigled into what purported to be a game of
soldiers, and before I knew what I was about I
was half-way through the Wars of the Roses.
At Christmas I got a present of (apparently) a
pot of jam. I opened it, and out jumped the
leaders of the Liberal Party, and I had to learn
their names. No matter how careful I am, I am
constantly being tricked in this way. Of course
it is too late now for anything to be done for me.
I am lost; and as they have got it all into me by

false pretences I am a sinik as well. There are, however, younger children to follow, and for their sakes I appeal to parents. I would particularly implore them, as they remember their own childhood in the happy pre-educational nurseries, to set their faces against the latest abomination, the gegraphical carpet, which is even worse than the zological doors, for there is no licking the paint off it.

The alphabetical biscuits are not the shabbiest. Each of them has a letter on it, which is meant to catch your eyes before you can get it into your mouth. With a little care, however, you can pop in the biscuits without looking, unless your nurse or mother insists on your saying the letter before she lets you eat it. There are mothers who do this; and if you give way at first, they have you into biscuits in one syllable in no time. The only safe course is to shut your eyes and be stubborn. It is no use looking one way and eating another, for unless you shut them you are bound to look at something, and you can't look anywhere in an educational nursery without being caught. Say you slide the biscuit in at the left side of your mouth and keep your eyes fixed on the wall to the right; the result is that you are learning pictorally who signed Magna Charta, and what was the beastly date of it.

It is very doubtful whether a biscuit, unless perhaps at bedtime, is worth all this bother. These biscuits are 'graded.' That is to say, you pass from alphabetical biscuits to biscuits in one, two, and even three syllables; and then there are names-of-countries biscuits. One would expect the biscuits to become bigger as they become more difficult, but they don't. I gave up biscuits at the second syllable, perferring to go into animal gingerbread. And then look at those instructional milk-mugs. Surely it is a little hard that a child cannot take a drink of milk without also absorbing the names of the many kinds of cows.

I know all about Shakespeare and Milton and Rare Bill Jonson, drat them. It is not my fault; it comes of not being surspicious. My little sister who brags that she will live two years after me because she is two years younger has a box of bricks that make into worldly houses on week-days and Westminster Abbey on Sundays. You get a picture of the Abbey on the lid, showing how to build the bricks, and it is good enough fun so long as you think it is nothing else. No sooner, though, have we built the Abbey than our guardians pounce and have us in that awful Poets' Corner. The royal ninepins are just as bad. As soon as we stick them up our governess asks who can tell her which is the fifth or the tenth Henry. You get only one mark for knocking him down but four if you can say when he was drowned in a bath of mulberry wine. The prize is varable. Sometimes it is a poetry lozenge, or it may be a toy for teaching you the months of the year. We are young and guileless, so no one has the sense to see that we are being taken advantage of except me.

There is a Latin proverb, which no boy should know before he is fourteen, about the Greeks being most to be kicked when they bring presents to you. But our own fathers and mothers are not a bit better than the Greeks about this, and I would strongly advise all children into whose hands this impeachument may fall not to accept a present from anybody without having a good look at it behind the door first. I got a ship on my last birthday that takes to pieces and packs away in a box. Do you think that was an honest present? It sounds like it; but it wasn't. If it hadn't been for that box I might not have known to this day how many ounces there are in a pound.

Children may be warned against squares, which are among the nastiest things I know of. Before taking them from anybody make sure that they don't squeak. If they do, and you take them, you are in for Equatorial Africa. I am, however, incline to think that the most invidiuous thing we have in our nursery is the money-box. The old style of money-box was plain and honest, and you could always get the pennies back with a knife. Ours, however, is a very different affair. It consists of a box with a donkey standing near it, and if you put a penny on the donkey's tail it kicks up one of its hind legs and knocks the penny into the box. It is a great joke to see the donkey doing this a few times, but there is no way of getting the money back, so of course it is a swindle. You may announce that we should know better; but we are innercent and at the mercy of designing parents. Why, if any of them were to see me writing these reflections, what do you think they would say? They would badger me till I told them what ink was composed of and what other ingreduents besides linen rags entered into the composition of paper. There is not, I suppose, anything I don't know, and if there is, father will be bringing it home on Saturday. I do wish I was growed up."

I DARESAY Greenwood had letters from parents saying they refused to believe that a child of six had written this paper with so many long words in it. I am sure Anon was never in an Educational Nursery, indeed though I knit my brows in thought I cannot recall his having in those days ever been in a nursery at all. He never had a nursery himself, I don't believe that the most genteel friend of his childhood ever had a nursery; it seems to me, looking back, that he was riotously happy without nurseries, without even a nana (but with some one better) to kiss the place when he bumped. The children of six he had met were, if boys, helping their father to pit the potatoes, and if girls, they were nurses (without knowing the word) to some one smaller than themselves. He came of parents who could not afford nurseries, but who could by dint of struggle send their daughters to boarding-schools and their sons to universities.

Perhaps Anon did meet in London some children of the nurseries, and found with surprise what care had to be taken of them at six years of age; that, for instance, there needed to be a tall fender to prevent their falling into the fire. Such children were something new in the world to him. Perhaps he studied them closely, perhaps just sufficiently to rip an article out of them. He may have made a call and his hostess have instructed the nurse to carry the eldest down very carefully so that the visitor might be gazed at with safety. On the other hand this article may have been evolved out of Anon's seeing an alphabetical biscuit in a shop-window.

Heigho, so long it is since I had a 'way' with children. I remember more vividly than most things the day I first knew it was gone. The blow was struck by a little girl, with whom I had the smallest acquaintance, but I was doing my best to entertain her when suddenly I saw upon her face the look that means, 'You are done with all this, my friend.' It is the cruellest, most candid look that ever comes into the face of a child. I had to accept it as final, though I swear I had a way with them once. That was among the most rueful days of my life.

CHAPTER XV

"WE have missed the publishing season again, not greatly to my surprise, for this is my fifth disillusionment. It would not do to mention his name; but he is world renowned, and seven years ago I admired him so much (as I do still) that he appointed me his biographer. He was an old man then, and infirm, so there was a sort of informal understanding between us that, alas, he would not last long. I worked night and day in the arrangement of his letters, autobiographical notes and other remains, forming them into a most interesting biography, which he was desirous to revise himself. For five years it has been ready for the Press; but he insists that the publication must be posthumous. He has had several illnesses; but he shakes them all off; and the publishers wrote to me last week saying he looks so sprightly that they have given him up for another year. Of course I admire him as much as ever, but at the same time this is evidently to be a splendid season for memoirs, and I have mouths to feed and little feet to shoe.

For these five years he has been engrossed in nothing but his health. Had he continued to increase his reputation there would have been nothing at which to murmur; but he has not even the interest in his reputation that he used to have. At his time of life most distinguished men are martyrs to insomnia, but he sleeps better now, he says, than for forty years; and he came back from his last tour abroad frolicking rather than leaning on his staff. One night in September of this year I saw him in the stalls of a theatre with an opera-glass at his eyes, which was surely a little brazen in a man who, seven years ago, distinctly stated to my grief and that of another (whom I could bring forward as a witness) that he had one foot in the grave. I don't cavil at his still being with us, I rejoice in it; but I do think that out of consideration for me he might remain studiously at home. Even as it is it would be painful to me to think that I had in a moment of irritation said one word against him. When the memoir does appear it will be found that he is the hero whom I have always worshipped.

In the meantime, as there is no immediate prospect of the biography's being published, let me say in justice both to him and myself that he is not blind to the awkward position in which his health has placed me. There are moments when he sympathizes with me keenly, and shows it by a pressure of the hand. Out of sheer kindness I have known him remark in conversation with me that he was not feeling so well to-day. On such occasions I could appreciate his motive; but the statement sent no thrill through me, for his face belied his words. He has looked at me apologetically, too, when others have remarked in my presence on his vigour; so that he is still, as I have always thought him, a man of feeling. Once or twice—not often, I am glad to say—I have been betrayed into talking a little bitterly of biographies prepared too soon, and then he has perhaps blustered. Legally, I admit frankly he is right in holding that I have no claim on him, and that I accepted the post at a certain risk. Yet this is scarcely a matter that should be looked at merely from the legal point of view. The question is whether the informal understanding I have already referred to left him absolutely a free man. So long as he treats me kindly I am willing not to press the point, and to rejoice in his vigour; but my outlook is a little saddened when he seems to forget, as he sometimes does; even openly exulting over me.

In the meantime the biography is suffering

in various ways. I pass over his comparative indifference to the work, though in my esteem for him I naturally desire that it should be as good as possible. A few years of leisure at the end of a laborious and distinguished career are neither here nor there (except to him and me); but a stately biography would keep him before the public for a sufficiency of months. However, if he will not stretch a point for my sake, I need not discuss the matter. What is perhaps more serious is that the book is losing both in freshness and truthfulness as a picture of this splendid man. He is becoming garrulous, and has told some of the best and most characteristic things in the book at his club. As any one knows, this means that the newspaper men get hold of the stories and telegraph them round the globe. For instance there was something about him, which he must have supplied himself, in a society paper last week that ruins my fifth chapter. Then there is his interview with Carlyle at Craigenputtock, which I had been trusting reviews would quote. He was in Dumfries many years ago, and drove to Craigenputtock to meet the sage, whom he did not happen to know personally. He thought, however, that his name would be sufficient introduction. On reaching the farm he saw Carlyle sitting on a dyke. The sage would not let him approach, saying he had never heard of him, and finally chased him round the duck pond. He learned afterwards from the schoolmaster that this was one of Carlyle's 'bad days,' and also that a labourer in the parish was paid by the genial author of 'Sartor Resartus' £5 per annum to take admiring visitors to another farm and pretend that it was Craigenputtock. Now all this is very interesting, and I would never have thought of mentioning it here did I not know that the London Correspondents will have it in a day or two. A friend of mine assures me that the subject of my biography has been telling the story at tea-parties, in which he now finds the greatest pleasure; and, furthermore, that he requests his audience not to let his indiscretion come to my ears. Clearly, therefore, my august friend is aware that he is wronging me and doing the biography harm; and it is obvious that if this kind of thing goes on the reviewers will find little that is new in the book.

Unless I largely re-write it, I may even be taken to task for misunderstanding my man. Until the last year or two he was almost a recluse, very reserved, seldom mixing in company, quite unknown except by his magnificent work to the general public. Now he is a club-man; he has been seen at flower-shows; he has insisted on

trying the switchback railway; his mantelshelf
is ornamented with cards of invitations to 'at
homes.' It is to me a matter of grave concern
that those who have met him only lately will find
it difficult to believe that I have known that noble
brain aright.

When I was appointed his biographer my
friends made much of me; but as year after
year passed without anything coming of it I have
taken a lower place in their estimation; others,
seeing that it is a sore subject, hasten to talk of
something else. They know that the fault is
not mine (nor do I call it his): but nevertheless
I suffer for it.

He has no longer the pleasure in my society
that he once had. He has become so lively that
he describes me to others as a heavy fellow. I
daresay that is true, but I do not take it to be
the real reason of his avoidance of me. I fear
that sometimes I cannot help looking reproachfully at him. He reads this as dumb suffering
in my eyes, and it annoys him. This is particularly noticeable when he is being treated for
one of the ailments that seem in the end to give
him new strength. Then he breaks out violently,
and says that I am a hypocrite when I express a
hope that he will soon be better. His servants
have told me in confidence that he shudders every

time he hears that I have been at the door in-quiring for him. Once we almost quarrelled. He had been confined to bed with a cold (he is all right again), and I went to the doctor's house to hear how he really was. He heard of this, and being unjust in his illness, the object of my devotion sent me a magazine containing an article on centenarians. This, I confess, pained me; and, forcing my way into his bedroom, I said more than I ought to have said. Never should I forget his greatness. Since then he is nervous if we are left alone together; but that is the only sign of shakiness I can find about him. As for the fickle public, some of them insist that the biography appeared years ago, and that they have read it."

THOUGH this article was entirely fanciful it sets me thinking of George Meredith and of the day he walked up and down in Flint Cottage reading it and mockingly assuming the leading rôle. I remember his putting the paper-knife into my hand to stab him with.

He was royalty at its most august to Anon, whose very first railway journey on coming to

George Meredith and J. M. Barrie

London was to Box Hill to gaze at the shrine. Whether Anon wore the Hat on this great occasion I cannot now remember. The Hat would certainly have been an encumbrance in the country, but as an honour to the man in whom he did take the most delight I hope he wore it. There is a grassy bank, or there was (for I go there no more), opposite the gate, and the little royal residence is only some twenty yards away. Even to Anon that day it seemed small but very royal. He sat on the grassy bank and quivered. Presently he saw a face at the window of a little sitting-room he was to be very familiar with in the hereafter. He knew whose face it was. Then the figure stood in the doorway, an amazing handsome man in grey clothes and a red necktie. He came slowly down the path towards the gate. It was too awful for Anon. He ran away. If the Hat was with him it must have been in his hand; he could not have run with it on his head. Meredith knew of this affair afterwards, and also of the store I set by the Hat, which made him throw back his head and laugh uproariously. He always insisted afterwards that I was wearing the Hat on that pilgrimage, and that what brought him down the path was to have a closer look at it and not at Anon. After his wont he paraphrased the in-

cident into vast proportions, and maintained that
he thought I was the first arrival for his funeral.

Something I wrote made him ask me to visit
him, and after that I was often at Flint Cottage
for stretches of time until he died in 1909. I
loved this man more every time I saw him. The
last time, when he was very frail, I said I thought
he had a better colour, and he replied with a
smile, 'Yes, a pretty green.' He was then too
hard of hearing to follow what you said unless
you were close to him, and while he talked of
women and wine and the winds his nurse, most
faithful but not in literary taste a Meredithian,
was telling me of his health and other matters.
'They assure me,' she said, with an affectionate
glance at him, 'that he has a wonderful knowledge of woman; all I can say is that I don't
think he knows one little thing about women.'
I felt that I was looking at a Shakespearian fragment. Morley, who was his executor, wanted
me to write his Life, but Meredith had told me
that he wished nothing of the kind to be done,
and in his last weeks he saw to it that bonfires
of his 'literary remains' should smoulder in his
garden. In any case there is no one less qualified
than I to write the Life of any one. I wrote a
few things of no account about him, and when
he died a little piece that I should like to insert

here. Had he been present he would certainly
have said that he saw me writing it on the grassy
bank, using the Hat as a desk:—

'All morning there had been a little gathering
of people outside the gate. It was the day on
which Mr. Meredith was to be, as they say,
buried. He had been, as they say, cremated.
The funeral coach came, and a very small thing
was placed in it and covered with flowers. One
plant of the wallflower in the garden would have
covered it. The coach, followed by a few others,
took the road to Dorking where, in familiar
phrase, the funeral was to be. In a moment or
two all seemed silent and deserted, the cottage,
the garden, and Box Hill.

'The cottage was not deserted, as They knew
who now trooped into the round in front of it,
their eyes on the closed door. They were the
mighty company, his children, Lucy and Clara
and Rhoda and Diana and Rose and Old Mel and
Roy Richmond and Adrian and Sir Willoughby
and a hundred others, and the shades of many
dogs, and they stood in line against the box-
wood, waiting for him to come out. Each of
his proud women carried a flower, and the hands
of all his men were ready for the salute. His
dogs were in commotion.

'In the room on the right, in an armchair

which had been his home for years—to many
the throne of letters in this country—sat an old
man, like one forgotten in an empty house.
When the last sound of the coaches had passed
away he moved in his chair. He wore grey
clothes and a red tie, and his face was rarely
beautiful, but the hair was white, and the limbs
were feeble, and the piercing eyes dimmed, and
he was hard of hearing. He moved in his chair,
for something was happening to him, old age
was falling from him. This is what is meant by
Death to such as he, and the company awaiting
knew. His eyes became again those of the eagle,
and his hair was brown, and the lustiness of
youth was in his frame, but still he wore the red
tie. He rose, and not a moment did he remain
within the house, for "golden lie the meadows,
golden run the streams," and "the fields and the
waters shout to him golden shouts." He flung
open the door, as They knew he would do who
were awaiting him, and he stood there looking
at them, a general reviewing his troops. They
wore the pretty clothing in which he had loved
to drape them; they were not sad like the
mourners who had gone, but happy as the forget-
me-nots and pansies at their feet and the barking
dogs, for they knew that this was his coronation
day. Only one was airily in mourning, as know-

ing better than the others what fitted the occasion,
the Countess de Saldar. He recognized her sense
of the fitness of things with a smile and a bow.
The men saluted, the women gave their flowers
to Dahlia to give to him, so that she, being the
most unhappy and therefore by him the most
beloved, should have his last word, and he took
their offerings and passed on. They did not go
with him, these, his splendid progeny, the ladies
of the future, they went their ways to tell the
whole earth of the new world for women which
he had been the first to foresee.

'Without knowing why, for his work was done,
he turned to the left, passing his famous cherry-
blossom, and climbed between apple-trees to a
little house of two rooms, whence many of that
noble company had sprung. It is the Chalet,
where he worked, and good and brave men will
ever bow proudly before it, but good and brave
women will bow more proudly still. He went
there only because he had gone so often, and this
time the door was locked; he did not know why
nor care. He came swinging down the path,
singing lustily, and calling to his dogs, his dogs
of the present and the past; and they yelped
with joy, for they knew they were once again to
breast the hill with him.

'He strode up the hill whirling his staff, for

which he had no longer any other use. His hearing was again so acute that from far away on the Dorking road he could hear the rumbling of a coach. It had been disputed whether he should be buried in Westminster Abbey or in a quiet churchyard, and there came to him somehow a knowledge (it was the last he ever knew of little things) that people had been at variance as to whether a casket of dust should be laid away in one hole or in another, and he flung back his head with the old glorious action, and laughed a laugh "broad as a thousand beeves at pasture."

'Box Hill was no longer deserted. When a great man dies—and this was one of the greatest since Shakespeare—the immortals await him at the top of the nearest hill. He looked up and saw his peers. They were all young, like himself. He waved the staff in greeting. One, a mere stripling, "slight unspeakably," R. L. S., detached himself from the others, crying gloriously, "Here's the fellow I have been telling you about!" and ran down the hill to be the first to take his Master's hand. In the meanwhile an empty coach was rolling on to Dorking.'

CHAPTER XVI

"FASCINATING as is the question, What is genius? recently propounded by an able writer, it has perhaps a more human interest when expressed in the personal form, 'Am I a genius?' I confess to having occasionally put the problem to myself. Sometimes I murmur it aloud, forgetting that my so-called friend Gilray is in the room, and he promptly answers No. Fortunately Gilray is dining out to-night, so this is an admirable opportunity for communing pleasantly on the matter.

The writer referred to says very truly that if we cannot easily decide what is Genius (henceforth to be called G in this paper), we can at least clear the ground by deciding what it is not. The more I seek to know myself the more certain do I feel that Carlyle was wrong in defining G as an infinite capacity for taking pains. Granting for the moment (in the blessed absence of Gilray) that I am a G, but leaving the natural bent of

175

my G an open question (for I have still to decide
whether I bend best as a philosopher, or a man
of letters, or by reason of indomitable practical
energy), my pre-eminence, I note (sparing myself
nothing), has not come through taking infinite
pains. Even Gilray would agree to this. More
satisfactory to me is the grudging distinction
made by Kenny Meadows between G and talent,
namely that G is power without effort, and talent
power with effort. I am inclined to think that
mine is power without effort. It is certainly
something without effort. I always like to dash
a thing off and be done with it. Of course where
you cannot do this it is creditable to you to make
the effort; but you ought clearly to understand
that this is talent. For my own part I have
never desired talent, and there seems to me something pathetic as well as praiseworthy in the way
Carlyle sat up through the long nights acquiring
power with effort. As an ambitious man he had
doubtless no other course open to him, though
G, lying on its back, cannot help smiling at
talent in its shirt-sleeves.

The writer referred to pertinently remarks of
the question before us, 'Am I a G?' that if the
response is genuine (as I hope mine is), it gives
a flash into the character of the person interro-
gated. 'If he will but give you the real thought

of his heart on this point, you can tell at once to what order of mind he belongs; whether to the contemplative or the imaginative, the purely intellectual, or the plainly practical.' Did this ingenious statement require proof it would be found in the case of Carlyle and myself; for he adopted the definition, 'An infinite capacity for taking pains,' while I lean to power without effort. There is an obvious danger here; as this means that a man is unconsciously biassed by the force of his own personality. Whether we are to attain to-night a true definition of G (which largely depends on how long Gilray stays away at dinner) it seems certain that the great mass of mankind are incapacitated for the search. Carlyle certainly was prejudiced; indeed, the most conclusive proof of this was not so much a definition drawn from his own personality (talent, I fear we must call it bluntly), as his incapacity to see that there are any other possible definitions, and that one of them may contain the truth. I am not prejudiced in that way. Naturally (for we all have our weaknesses), I like to think that G is power without effort, or, rather, that power without effort is G; but I am prepared to admit that I may be wrong. If we are to inquire into this matter at all, let us do it with open minds. If you prefer to think that G is power with effort

M

instead of without effort, then by all means acknowledge Carlyle a G and leave me out.

Just as we can decide what is not G, though we are unable to say what is, we can say who are not Gs without fixing easily upon who are. Thus I know that Gilray is not a G. The mere suggestion that he is would raise a smile on the face of all. Does this, however, help us? What is it in Gilray that makes us so sure of him? Is he lacking in certain qualities or powers which, whether they make G or not, are to be found in, say, me. I am afraid so. When he attempts to argue on the subject of G, he gets out of his depth; also he falls asleep as soon as he goes to bed; and he is invariably bright and cheerful. With me it is very different. I am never in my element until I reach deep water. The unfathomable sea of thought in which Gilray would drown seems to buoy me up. While he, not caring whether he is a G or not so long as he gets a good night's rest, falls asleep, I lie awake busy with the problems of my personality. As a result he gets through more work in the daytime than I do, for I require to rest on the sofa during the afternoon. By that time my brain is tired out. Lastly, I am by no means the invariably cheerful person he is. He is always the same, ever the characteristic of a mediocrity, while my moods

are as changeable as hoary ocean. There are
times when I am the best of company, when my
wit sparkles and cuts. At other times I walk
in the shadows. Then let no Gilray speak to me
(I wish he would remember this), for I am in a
world of my own. Suppose I am ruminating
with the mighty dead. The slightest thing seems
to send me out of the one mood into the other,
such as being contradicted. In Carlyle this dark
mood showed itself in irritability, but I am never
irritable even with Gilray.

Admirable though the paper which suggests
these reflections is, it is perhaps unnecessarily
despondent, there being one way in which we
may arrive at a definition of G that has escaped
the writer. He is correctly of opinion that G is
not a word of different meanings, but rather
'some peculiar mental quality in common between the soldier and the poet.' The difficulty
is to find what that quality is; but I think I can
manage it. We must start with the assumption
(I consider it no more) that I am a G, and then
go over the various definitions, striking out as
false those which do not apply. In this way we
at once get rid of the Carlylean definition. It
having been granted by you that I may be a G,
it is even more certain that I have no definite
capacity for taking pains. Already, therefore,

we have made an advance. The common creed
with the rabble, as our writer points out, is that
G is synonymous with success. I have, however,
been far less successful than Gilray, so that this
creed obviously leaks. Indeed every one of my
acquaintance who pretends to G has been unsuccessful. Of course one may be unsuccessful
without being a G. Still this excludes another
common view. Also we may safely disregard
the business man's theory that G is 'a large
general capacity specially turned into a particular
direction.' I have taken care not to turn my
capacity into any special groove; indeed, I have
tried several directions for it at different times
and given them all up; which seems to favour
the belief that G rebels against restraint. Nor
is G 'a noble enthusiasm constraining the person
possessed by it to action of an heroic kind'; for
though I am momentarily enthusiastic, no action
comes of it, the reverse being the case with such
as Gilray. In this way we shut out all the definitions but two: namely, power without effort, to
which I must plead guilty, and 'a creative working
in strict accordance with nature and the fitness
of things.' I am not sure what this means, but
I feel I have it; it was probably also in men of
such opposite types as Napoleon and Words-
worth. Yes; there can be no G where there is

no creative power. Gilray's observation upon this is that I have created nothing. Nevertheless I consider that if——

However, I hear his garrulous footstep on the stair, so I must dissemble."

THE Gilray of this blackguardly effusion is once more my great friend Gilmour of the frontispiece, who may, it is crushing to me to reflect, have limned his noble sketch of Anon that very evening. On re-examining the sketch one notes nevertheless that he has omitted the G as well as the Hat.

In this article Anon makes so much use of his friend that in a sense they are collaborators, though Anon doubtless pocketed both the guineas. To this extent he often collaborated. Nevertheless real collaboration and how it is done still puzzles me, though I essayed it twice with two of my best friends, Marriott Watson and Conan Doyle. In both cases it was on a play, one being 'Richard Savage' and the other a comic opera called 'Jane Annie.' For the last score of years, and probably much longer, I could have sworn that 'Savage' was my first long play, but the other day a MS. of one I had

completely forgotten wandered into an auction
sale under the title of 'Bohemia.' It had been
written in my university days, and I could not
believe in its genuineness till they showed me
the title-page. They wanted me to read it all,
but oh no. The title-page contained one amusing
item; a scene is laid, obviously in all sincerity,
in 'A glade in Brighton,' which shows that he
knew at that time as much about Brighton as
he knew about Bohemia. This work was never
presented, however, while 'Savage' was produced
for a matinée at the expense of the authors. My
recollection is that I wrote bits in Scotland and
Marriott wrote bits in London, and that we then
re-wrote each other's bits. It was a dark and
gloomy affair and my only stage adventure into
the historical; but it was graced by a prologue
in verse from Henley, and we were so anxious
not to be diffuse, after the manner of beginners,
that we polished off the love scene in about
twenty lines. This was the only occasion on
which I ever took an 'author's call,' and we were
derided by a ribald Press as 'the long and the
short of it,' because of my collaborator's unfortunately great height. I dreamt on the night
of production that Conan Doyle was producing
a play across the street on the same afternoon,
and that I stood at the door of my theatre waiting

vainly for a public to come in while he stood waiting similarly at his. At last I darted across and dragged him in to see 'Savage,' its only spectator.

'Jane Annie' was a dreadful failure. I had undertaken to do it 'off my own bat' for the D'Oyly Carte's, and went into hiding to escape it, was discovered and brought back and allowed to introduce a collaborator, who was Doyle. (I sat with him on the seashore at Aldeburgh when he decided to kill Sherlock Holmes.) He wrote some good songs, I thought, for 'Jane Annie,' but mine were worthless and I had no musical sense. Also he was so good-natured that if we lost him at rehearsals he was sure to be found in a shrouded box writing a new song for some obscure member of the company. They had only to plead with him, 'I have nothing to say, Mr. Doyle, except half a dozen lines in the first act,' when he would reply, 'Oh, my poor chap, too bad,' and retire into a box, from which he emerged almost instantly with a song. As for me, a boy got into the play merely to gather boots from bedroom doors, but he became the one person I was interested in, and so was soon the leading character, to the indignation of the stars. On the first night at the end a youthful friend came into our box, and Doyle expressed my feelings in saying to him reprovingly, 'Why did you not cheer?' but I also sympathized with our visitor when he answered plaintively, 'I didn't like to, when no one else was doing it.'

I say that I have no ear for music, and indeed it is so true that I have only once been to the opera. It was one of the great operas, magnificently done, with Melba in it, and almost thirty years have elapsed since then, but I still shudder at its tedium. Madame Melba was very nearly, like myself, a native of Kirriemuir. She was born soon after her parents had left there for Melbourne. A few years ago, though we had never met, I thought this an excuse, on finding that we were both inmates of a London nursing home, to send a message to her that I would like very much to go downstairs to see her if she would promise not to sing to me; and she replied that she would love it if I promised not to read any of my works to her. On that understanding we had a happy time.

The D'Oyly Cartes were delightful people to work with. Years afterwards I was wandering on a Highland moor with the late Lord Esher, and in the intimacy that shrewd air creates, one of us (I am not sure now which one) said to the other, 'If you will tell me who is the most remarkable woman you have known I shall tell you

Agreement this day, 6 Dec 19
03 between J. M. Barrie of Leinster-
Corner of the one part and John
LL Davies of 23 Kensington Park
Gardens of the other part. WHEREAS
J. M. Barrie (to be hereafter called
the aforesaid) is part-author of a
play named Little Mary, of which
John LL Davies is part-author
of the other part. the aforesaid
undertakes to pay to John LL
Davies ~~the sum~~ (to be hereafter
called the above-mentioned) the
SUM of ONE Halfpenny per diem
during the run of the play.

Signed
J. M. Barrie
John LL. Davies

An agreement between collaborators

who is mine.' Then we both said Mrs. D'Oyly Carte.

I remember now being in one other collaboration. It has been sometimes referred to in the Press, but incorrectly. While I was writing my play of 'Little Mary' I said to a small boy of six or seven who was sitting up in bed eating chocolates, 'If you eat so many chocolates you will be sick to-morrow,' to which he replied promptly, 'I shall be sick to-night.' This got into the play, and recognizing his child, he claimed his rights, with the result that I had to draw up the enclosed deed of collaboration.

CHAPTER XVII

"SANDFORD AND MERTON"——MEREDITH AGAIN
——THE 'SCOTS OBSERVER'——W. E. HENLEY AND
CHARLES WHIBLEY——OSCAR WILDE AND JOHN
SILVER'S CRUTCH

"(a) *Mr. Barlow's Sense of Propriety.*

HAVING partaken of his matutinal meal on Bank Holiday, Mr. Barlow, with his goloshes strapped to his umbrella, summoned his pupils, Sandford and Merton, similarly strapped, and taking them by the hand conducted them to the beach where, shaking his head to the invitation of the waves, he courteously but firmly refused to look further at the ocean.

HARRY. It would, I frankly admit, be idle on my part and on that of my fellow pupil to pretend that we are wholly cognizant of the doubtless valid causes which induce you thus publicly to cast such a slight upon the sea.

Mr. Barlow bowed his head dejectedly and, slightly bending his left leg, seemed to be on the point of speaking when he caught sight of a barefooted man enveloped in a towel. With a shudder he resumed his original attitude.

186

TOMMY. This is to us indescribably disturbing, and perhaps not the less so because we
are painfully aware that our grief must be
due to not wholly excusable ignorance. I
cannot doubt that should your sombre
thoughts remind you of a tale which, as we
have not yet heard it, you will now proceed
to narrate, our bosoms will immediately
palpitate with some worthy emotion.

HARRY. I shall content myself momentarily
with pointing out that the place, the hour
and the concourse of promenaders are alike
adapted for the inculcation of a moral
lesson.

MR. BARLOW. My ambition has ever been to
train your young minds by means of noble
sentiments fitly expressed, and therefore I
do not hesitate to inform you that I cannot
look upon the sea without a sense of shame.

TOMMY. Allow me, sir, a moment to com-
mune. Your passion for social purity—but
I see that Harry wishes to speak.

HARRY. Nay, Tommy, I cannot interrupt you.

TOMMY. Excuse me, my dear friend, you were
about to say——?

HARRY. What you, Tommy, would have said
better. May I hazard the assertion, sir,
that since you joined the Society for Blushing

at Human Figures on Hoardings, even the sight of the sea is to your pure mind impure?

MR. BARLOW. It is even so.

TOMMY. Without implying for a moment, esteemed sir, that I can detect impurity as quickly as you do, I may say that since you addressed us on this subject I have discovered it in placards which hitherto I had passed by as inoffensive.

MR. BARLOW. The wickedness of this world is only known when we think of it much and look for it everywhere.

HARRY. In the hour which by your advice we devote to relaxation, Tommy and I have for the past week been examining the hoardings with, I venture to say, admirable result.

TOMMY. Many of the pictorial advertisements when regarded without reflection are innocent enough, but when studied with the eye of knowledge are exceedingly improper.

HARRY. Yet to our humiliation be it said we still enjoy, in the lightness of our hearts, gazing at the sea and even cautiously entering it.

MR. BARLOW. Though you are apt pupils you do not perceive that an object itself may be harmless and yet suggestive. I have no quarrel with the province of Aquarius as

such, but when an individual is as pure in
mind as I am he is so sensitive to impropriety that he sees it where others do not.
To you, for instance, in your present incomplete stage of pupildom, a piece of
string is inoffensive, but to me it is an
article that might be used as a garter, and
I blush at sight of it.

TOMMY. I never thought of that.

HARRY. Nor I.

MR. BARLOW. You have not let your minds
dwell on the improper as I have done. Now,
as for the sea——

TOMMY. One moment, sir, Harry and I have
for so long thoughtlessly regarded the sea
with pleasure that before you make us
acquainted with its impropriety we should
like to take a last look at it.

The two pupils then took a last look at the
sea.

HARRY. Now, sir, we shall be beholden to
you, as ever, if you will tell us why the sea
is improper.

MR. BARLOW. I am disappointed in you both.
Can you observe that row of bathing
machines, and still ask me why it is impossible to look at the sea without a sense
of shame?

TOMMY and HARRY (turning their backs to the ocean). Take us away, sir, we beg of you.

(b) *Mr. Barlow's Sense of Citizenship.*

In the evening Mr. Barlow's home with its cosy curtains and bright lamp presented such a picture of domestic bliss that Harry was calling Tommy's attention to the many advantages enjoyed by them under the roof of their revered preceptor, when the silence of the night was broken suddenly by the cry 'Another Hor'ble Murder in Whitechapel.'

Mr. Barlow, who had been rotating slowly by the fire (for the night was chilly), bounded to the window.

'Shockin' mutilation!'

His pupils followed him.

'Details more revoltin' than ever!'

MR. BARLOW. Tommy, get a paper. Quick.

The maid, Jane, however, reached the door first. All the doors in the street opened simultaneously as if they had one handle, and there was a general rush toward the newsboy. Mr. Barlow returned to the hearthrug, and after a few moments' reflection thus addressed his young friends:

MR. BARLOW. This deplorable news fills me

with inexpressible sadness. I hoped that we had heard the last of these horrible barbarities in the modern Babylon.

TOMMY. When we have regard to the circumstances that have called them forth the words 'modern Babylon' are obviously well chosen, and I shall at present merely indicate my cordial sympathy with your remarks, leaving for some future occasion that corroboration which, however desirable, would scarcely be felicitous at a time when we are all—for I may venture to speak for Harry also—more or less prostrated by the crushing intelligence.

HARRY. Jane is a long time in getting the paper.

TOMMY. It is conceivable that the amount of money in her possession is not sufficient to appease the rapacity of the newsvendor. If, sir, I had a sixpence——

MR. BARLOW. My beloved pupils, I see with pain that you have acquired an appetite for horrors, and I implore you to kill it. Only a sense of Citizenship induces me reluctantly to read these distressing details which I cannot contemplate with equanimity. Jane is certainly a long time, and if you think that a sixpence——

At this moment a roar of execration filled the street, followed by a clatter as if perhaps of a small humorist pursued by a disappointed public. Mr. Barlow's brows contracted. Then the door flung open and Jane entered in tears. 'There is no murder,' she wailed, 'it is all a wicked hoax.' Tommy brought the window down with a slam. Harry put his knuckles in his eyes. Mr. Barlow glowered at Jane as if she had defrauded him. Gloom settled on the room. There were similar scenes of Citizenship all down the street. Yes, it is high time that Jack the Ripper was caught."

THE appearance in it of the shadow of Jack the Ripper dates this paper, which was one of a series about the famous Mr. Barlow. It appeared with one or two others that follow in the 'Scots Observer,' and so is of a slightly later date than most of our book's contents. The 'Scots Observer,' under W. E. Henley's editorship, was started in Edinburgh in 1888, and I had a contribution in the first number and in many another. The first one was called 'The Lost Works of George Meredith,' and the works were

John Silver as an editor

(*from a painting by William Nicholson*)

three comparatively short stories (including the
lovely 'Chloe') and his fine essay on Comedy,
which had all been lying forgotten for ten years
between the covers of a dead magazine. My
article is of no value, save that my howking out
of the 'lost works' led to their publication in
book form, Meredith merely shrugging his con-
sent, though he had a good word to say for
'Chloe.' It was at a time of his life when he
regarded his lack of readers with a gay equanimity,
very different from those early days in which he
told me he used to run round Hyde Park three
times daily to get away from his troubled self.
He read portions of his later works to me in the
famous chalet at the top of his garden, and I
remember his saying that 'Richard Feverel' was
the only novel of his that in its youth reached
a second edition, some kindly readers having
shouted that it was vastly improper. He admitted
on one occasion that he thought 'Beauchamp's
Career' was his best novel, but that may have
only been in a mood of the moment. When I
spoke of Rhoda Fleming as among my favourite
heroines he said, disappointed, 'Surely you like
Dahlia better,' and I did from that hour.

The 'Scots Observer' (published in Edinburgh
by Constable, Walter Blaikie the shining head
thereof), afterwards 'National Observer,' was the

most gaily brilliant weekly of its day, and had the
endearing capacity of not being wise in its own
interest. Charles Whibley was Henley's right-
hand man and probably the journal's greatest
pride and terror. Charles had the tenderest
heart, or thereabout, that I have known, and was
extremely testy if you said so. You might read
him and conclude that if he got his way he would
by violent means reduce the population to a
handful. He liked to think he was such a one,
but the heart 'would keep breaking through'
and show him up. He was a scholar and, I
think, wrote, when not on the war-path, the best
English of his day. He was assistant editor;
and the staff, if the contributions can be so called,
was sufficiently scintillating to kill any journal.
Meredith, if my memory serves, never wrote in
it, but our other great one, Hardy (I did not
know him in those days, and am now undecided
as to which was the greater of the two), found
a home in the 'Scots Observer' for a chapter of
'Tess,' which the paper it appeared in serially
was afraid to print. The same paper, I remember,
shied at the scene in which Angel Clare carries
the dairymaids in his arms through the water,
and our immortal had to put them into a wheelbarrow.

I met Henley first in Edinburgh in one of his

most delicious moments, often repeated. The
stalwart burly man (as he was till he stood up)
was sitting at a piano playing impromptu music
to his child of three or so, the loveliest of little
girls, who sometimes as he played sat on the
piano till she fell into his lap, and sometimes
danced round the instrument and under it and
over me. I got the name of Wendy from her
for one of my characters—it was the nearest she
could reach to calling me Friend. Henley could
not cross a room without his crutch, and he
would stand for hours leaning on the back of a
chair with his coat off. Such was the glamour
of him to young men that you would sometimes
find a number of them listening to him, all unaware that they were leaning on the backs of
chairs with their coats off. He was a splendidly
ironic, bearded man, and John Silver was Steven-
son's idea of Henley taken to piracy. It was
Henley's crutch that Silver threw to clinch an
argument, and thus also did Henley throw it, as
I have seen. On this occasion the subject of
discussion was merely literary, the scene was the
steps of a London café, and the opponent was
Oscar Wilde, a very courteous opponent too, but
he was neatly pinned by that javelin.

Once I went to call on Henley quite prepared
to have the javelin cast at me. It was when he

had written a magazine article about R. L. S. that caused much talk at the time, and I knew that Henley thought I was the only one of his circle who regretted it. However, as we had to have the matter out or cease to meet, I advanced upon his flat in Battersea prepared to have the stave dirl in my ribs. He was certainly threatening at first, but contrite by and by, and before I left, without a scar, he was talking as of yore about 'dear Louis.' Uproarious discussion, with personalities hurtling about like little staves, was his way of taking physical exercise, this man who should have been a viking, and of whom nigh every part had been opened by the surgeons as one may double back a book. When he thundered a red light came into his eye, which so entranced you that you forgot it might be a danger signal. He thundered at all of us, especially if he loved us, as he usually did. It was Kipling, I think, who presented him with a punching ball, after first writing all our names on it. Meredith said to me of Henley's criticisms: 'He puts a crown on my head with one hand and buffets me in the stomach with the other.' He was like that, this 'W. G.' of letters, for thus only could he play rough games, sail ships, climb mountains, lead troops; he had emotions that boiled over, he roared with joy when he found writing to his

liking sent in by the young, and every day for
the last years of his life he woke to more physical
pain than the day before.   I never heard him
mention it.   The lovely child, of whom there is
a painting by Charles Furze, died when she was
about five; one might call it a sudden idea that
came to her in the middle of her romping.

CHAPTER XVIII

"A BLASTY night it was in Greenock on Thursday last, but we would only let ourselves be blown in one direction for a' that: into the Town Hall, to wit, where the Burns Dinner was 'on,' Mr. J. M. Barrie in the chair. I have not read Mr. Barrie's books, but I wanted to ask him about that tobacco.

I didn't.

We, or at least I, had looked to see a jovial Scot, full of merry quirk, rollicking, gay. I can't quite get the adjective that hits off Mr. Barrie, but I'll take my oath it is none of these. He fascinated me in a sense, and this is the faithful, though doubtless bold, record of my observations.

I was introduced to him, and we both held out our hands: having shaken his, I let go. His remained in the air, as if the ceremony was new to him. Several others were introduced, and he gave to all his hand to do what they liked with it. This being over he placed it by his side. We

198

then adjourned with unwonted solemnity to the
hall where dinner was to be served.

On the way I had time to sum up my impres-
sions. He was evidently anxious to please. The
way in which the arm shot out, like a pirate
lugger from its hiding-place, was proof of this.
The natural solemnity of his face is a little startling
to one who has come out to dine, but there is no
doubt that he made several gallant efforts to be
jolly. I noticed this, not only in the anteroom
but throughout the evening. When a joke was
made you could see him struggling, not with his
face alone, to laugh heartily. It was as if he
tugged the strings that work the organs of
risibility, but either the strings were broken or
he had forgotten to bring the organs. Only
once did he manage a genuine smile, but some
of us forgot ourselves and cheered, and it fled.
So far as I could see he found it beneath the
table. He had dived after his programme, I
think, and while below must have done something to his face akin to what the lady does when
she darts away with a crooked bonnet, and comes
back with it straight. Our cheering did not
offend him. He took it in the spirit in which
it was meant. But he was chiefly engaged in
keeping the so-called smile there. My wife has
pigeons on which she sets store; when one of

them alights on her head, she stands still and
calls to me to look at the beautiful sight. So
did Mr. Barrie sit hugging his smile. He was
even afraid to let it know that he knew it was
there. He might, so careful was he, have been
balancing something on his head. But as I say,
it fled. It was probably some other's smile that
had mistaken its owner.

When he entered the hall they stood up and
cheered. He cast a swift glance at the door, and
seemed to be meditating flight, but so many were
following behind that the way was blocked. Then
he affected deafness; at all events he looked before
him so stolidly that our palms stole away from
each other, ashamed of themselves. On his table
was a large epergne full of flowers. I saw him
move his chair stealthily, inch by inch, until he
was fairly behind this epergne. On the left and
right he shut himself in as far as possible with
bottles and cruets. He then settled down for a
jolly evening.

I was too far away to hear what he said when
he engaged in conversation. Obviously he was
very anxious to be sociable, for when those near
spoke to him he listened with an attention that
must have been painful to them if, as is probable,
they were only speaking of the weather. Sometimes it seemed to be a good story, for they

Out of the night that covers me,
  Black as the Pit from pole to pole,
I thank whatever gods there be
  For my unconquerable soul.

In the fell clutch of circumstance
  I have not winced nor cried aloud.
Under the bludgeonings of chance
  My head is bloody, but unbowed.

Beyond this place of wrath & tears
  Looms but the Horror of the Shade,
And yet the menace of the years
  Finds & shall find me unafraid.

It matters not how strait the gate,
  How charged with punishments the scroll
I am the master of my fate:
  I am the captain of my soul.

1875

William Ernest Henley

A Henley MS.

laughed, and he flung himself back in his chair
and waggled his head and slapped his knee and
went through all the mechanical business that
accompanies a laugh but is as a suit of clothes
without a man in them when, as in his case, the
laugh itself won't come. He might have been
called at such a time the photograph of a laugh
—a laugh with no inside to it.

The man who got most out of him was the
head waiter, to whom (this should go into the
minute-book of the club) he said, 'Clear,' 'Cod,'
'Mutton,' 'Haggis,' 'Roederer,' 'No thank you.'
His favourite remark is 'H'm,' with which he
expresses surprise, thankfulness, indignation,
delight, grief. He also asks questions with it,
and he has a 'H'm' that is final.

I never saw a man more interested in our
Burns Dinner programme. It is illustrated, and
the artists should be told how he examined their
handiwork. Again and again he seized the programme to have another look at it. He tried
the pictures at a distance and close to him, and
read the letterpress beneath with as much affection as if it cured everything. Round the room
his eyes would wander; then back to the programme they scuttled like a mouse to its hole.

He proposed the toast of the Queen in those
words.

He had to call upon the various speakers and singers, and as soon as he had uttered their names, he fell back with the recoil.

His own health was proposed, and we sung determinedly that he was a jolly good fellow. When we asked each other who could deny it, he sat and scowled. His speech in reply consisted of fifty words at least, but it was probably intended to be of a confidential nature, for it never crossed the table; and though it has been repeated to me, I scorn to betray a secret.

When it was all over he told some of us that he had not enjoyed himself so much for a long time. He seemed so anxious we should think him a jovial character that we responded heartily. Then he passed round his hand again, and when we had returned it to him, he said 'H'm' in his merriest way. That was the finish, for when we were fighting for our coats he slipped away like a burglar. I distinctly heard some one running along the otherwise silent street, but it may— it may—have been a street boy."

FEW suspected that Mr. Anon wrote this article, which as usual was anonymous, and Henley was

upbraided by my well-wishers for its publication
in the 'Scots Observer.' Some of the Press even
took up my defence, and it was the 'Westminster' (I think) which said that he had obviously
quarrelled with me and this was his characteristic
but contemptible revenge. I urged him to name
the guilty person, but he enjoyed the situation
too much for that. It was true, though, that I
had presided at the Greenock dinner referred to.
This must have been my first public appearance
in any chair, for in the days of Mr. Anon I was
so afraid of oratory that rather than make a speech
I would have fled the country.

This is not, alas, the only thing of the kind
that he who was once Mr. Anon has perpetrated.
I was in New York at the beginning of the war
on a matter not unconnected with it, and various
persons (including Mr. Roosevelt) drew my attention to a severely candid article about me in the
'New York Times.' It was called 'Barrie at
Bay,' and purported to be an interview with my
valued servant, Brown. Brown brought me a
copy and swore that he had never given any such
interview. The thing is much too long to reprint
in full, but it had its day, and I still possess that
copy. 'As our reporter entered Sir James Barrie's
hotel room by one door,' it begins, 'the next door
softly closed. "I sprang into the corridor," the

reporter continues, "and had just time to see him fling himself down the elevator. Then I understood what he had meant when he said on the telephone that he would be ready for me at 10.30."'

The reporter apparently found Brown, however, who discussed me in a way that afterwards astounded himself. He showed my pipe, but under pressure explained, 'That is the interview pipe. When we decided to come to America Sir James said he would have to be interviewed and that it would be wise to bring something with us for the interviewers to take notice of. So he told me to buy the biggest pipe I could find as he was no smoker. . . .' 'It has the appearance of having been smoked,' the reporter pointed out. 'I blackened it for him,' the faithful fellow replied.

Brown also supplied some interesting details about my works, less inaccurate than may be thought. 'He forgets them all,' said Brown. 'There is this Peter Pan foolishness, for instance. I have heard people talking to him about that play and mentioning parts in it they liked, and he tried to edge them off the subject; they think it is his shyness, but I know it is because he has forgotten the bits they are speaking about. Before strangers call on him I have seen him reading one of his own books hurriedly so as to be able to talk about it if that is their wish. But he gets mixed up, and thinks that the little minister was married to Wendy.'

Here is something to my credit. So anxious was President Wilson to have every one in America, including visitors, 'neutral' about the war that the reporter found I had enjoined Brown to be neutral on all other subjects as well, 'to express no preferences on matters of food, for instance, and always to eat oysters and clams alternately, so that there can be no ill-feeling. Also to walk in the middle of the street lest he should seem to be favouring either side-walk, and to be very cautious about admitting that one building in New York is higher than another. I assured him that the Woolworth Building was the highest, but he replied politely that he was sure the President would prefer him to remain neutral.'

In a final quotation Brown seems to have risen almost to the dignity of a prophet. 'It was pleasant to find that Brown has not a spark of sympathy with those who say that because Germany has destroyed art treasures in Belgium and France the Allies should retaliate with similar rudeness if they reach Berlin. He holds that if for any reason best known to themselves (such as the wish for a sunnier location) the Hohenzollerns should by and by vacate their present residence, a nice villa should be provided for them, and that all the ancestral statues in the Sieges-Allee should be conveyed to it intact and perhaps put up in the back garden. There the Junkers could drop in of an evening on the way home from their offices and chat pleasantly of old times.'

I have said that Roosevelt was among those deceived by this sketch. He was an entrancing personality, but such a talker that, though I spent a day with him at Oyster Bay on a mission connected with the war, I could not, as the saying goes, get in a word. The last I saw of him he was running and talking alongside the little carriage that took me to the station. Gradually we out-distanced his voice.

The copy of this old article I now possess reached me curiously enough from Arctic regions whither it was sent me by Stefansson, the famous explorer. I did not know him then (and I wish I knew him now), but it had somehow reached him among the eternal snow and he sent it to me in London thinking I had probably not seen it. Brown and I have sometimes discussed this article and wondered who could have written it. That is all very well, but how am I now to be able to present him with a copy of this book?

As for being 'interviewed,' my only boast is that I was never interviewed in my life.

CHAPTER XIX

"HEROES in fiction are longer this year than ever.
I take the average to be six feet two, which is
three-quarters of an inch longer than for the
preceding nine months. May I ask you lady
novelists when is this to stop? Why have you
never tried a short hero? It has been established
since the time of William Rufus that short men
have souls, are subject to impression from the
other sex, are eligible for clubs, and marry as
openly as their longer brethren. Why must they
be inadmissible? That short men figure in your
novels I, of course, know, but they are only there
that the hero may look over their heads. Two
young men constantly appear together in your
opening pages, and we know which is to be the
hero as soon as we have their measurements.
'The shorter of the two,' you begin, and at once
you have written his epitaph: 'Much respected
but not long enough.' It is permitted him to be
a good son and amorous, but never may he

gather her up or bite her in the neck. The shorter man may have wealth, in which case, my poor fellow, you will have to die and leave it to the lady. I know what you novelists will reply: that for the work a hero has to do a long man is necessary. You are referring to the bull, the mill-pond, the runaway carriage-horses, the fire, and the chalk-pit. I don't ask you to do without these, for I understand they are the load all your tribe must carry, but I see no reason why you should not try occasionally a short sturdy man. Short men are as quick on their legs as long ones, and could as easily snatch her from the bull. The mere fact of his waterproof being of a smaller size than the long man's need not prevent his flinging it round the animal's head. Why should it always be the longest spectator who dives after her? Short men can swim. A stout young hero, though short, could throw himself at runaway horses; he could run up the ivy of the burning house at least as quickly as a long fellow, whose legs (however dark you may keep this) would really be in the way; if his horse is short to suit, there is no reason why he should not overtake the lady's palfrey just as it is about to leap into the chalk-pit.

You smile at me as an outsider, who has forgotten the hero's most important qualification.

I have not forgotten it, nor shall I attempt to make light of it. I am aware that when he has vanquished the bull, the horses, the mill-wheel, and the tongues of flame, he has only waxed the floor for action. He must next convey her to a place of safety. There is the rub for the short man. Yet there must be a knack of carrying her which a short man could acquire with a few lessons as well as his betters. Also he need not carry her so very far. Why tell the actual distance? But, you say, she would know wherein he was wanting when he asked her the question that has been asked hundreds of thousands of times, yet is ever new. I forget what the question is, but why should not he know? He could even elongate himself for the moment. As he gathers her up and showers hot kisses on her you imply that he will gasp sooner than his long friend. Rightly considered, however, would not this prove him a truer hero than that other who gathers her as easily as he lights a Regalia Rothschild Havana? Surely the more he pants the grander the figure he presents.

Now we come to your heroines, and alas we must also chide you about them. I mean for the way in which, when Long Legs coldly leaves the lady, she rolls in agony along the floor. Heroines have always tended to cast themselves upon the floor in supreme moments, but they are rolling on it this year. In real life women, however lovely, and however long he is in the legs, are surely not quite so regardless of their persons and their garments.

I notice that she is nine times in ten a married woman, perhaps to give her an acquaintance that cannot be expected from the sweetest maiden, with rugs and carpets and battered floors. The most extraordinary thing about her and her husband, the Earl, is that they are madly, wildly, screamingly in love, but neither knows it about the other. She discovers as they leave the church that he has married her for her money (the sort of thing only the short fellows do); or he discovers that some other long one once saved her from the sinking ship, and after that the twain hate, hate, hate. They meet, however, at dances in their own house, and in the conservatory he takes her by the throat, with the wild hoarse passion of long ones, and asks her to dance with him, her husband, once. She draws her figure up until like him she almost dents the ceiling, and implies with her ripe hair in his eyes that if he dares to touch her waist she will change its place on her person. No sooner has the door closed on him than she moans 'Dicky, my Dicky,' and begins to roll across the floor. Back and

forward she rolls, back and forward, and any
shorter man's heart would be touched to see her
thus. Dicky, however, does not see her; we
are not always told what he is doing on these
occasions, but he has probably quickly kicked off
his shoes and found solace in measuring himself
in his stocking soles. The Dickies always
measure themselves in their stocking soles, an
extra fling at shorter men who before measuring
put on their boots.

There is not much told about the domestics
(except the male ones) in these novels, but they
must be in the background, and they are capable
maids too, such as you authoresses perhaps sigh
for in vain yourselves. For long hours they
must be kept sweeping the rooms where the
heroine is to roll, so that she may do it without
ruining her confection. The floors must be
padded or some sharp ear would hear her fall.
Yet though the proficient may roll softly it must
wear out the carpets in time, which entails heavy
after-hours' work on the toilers who make carpets.
There is always some member of the working
classes who suffers for the rollings of the aristo-
cracy.

The girls who are the wives of earls (for whatever the length of him may be she is still his
wife) can afford to dress extravagantly. Know-

ing their ways their maid has doubtless a change of garments always in readiness, and no doubt she benefits by the rolling, for she presumably gets their bursting gowns. On the whole, therefore, the more her ladyship rolls the better for the poorer classes.

I would point, however, to two kinds of readers to whom her behaviour is a little trying. First, there are the readers of her own sex, gentlewomen but comparatively poor, who in the end have to put up with men of five feet six. They try to copy the aristocrats of the floor, and I ask you to conceive the effect upon the purse of an ordinary professional man of a daughter who takes to rolling. She would have to put off her roll (thus spoiling the frenzy) till she hurriedly changed into a last year's frock, or she must limit herself to one roll in a season. It is said that whether titled or damned, young ladies prefer one big dance to ever so many little ones, and in the same way perhaps they would rather roll once in silk than weekly in merino. If the readers were young wives like the heroine, not so wealthy but just as fond of a bit of romance, their case would be still more parlous, for they might roll their husbands out of house and home in three months. Your heroines have no responsibility, they have housekeepers and that sort of thing instead; and their husband, the long Earl, can grow hoarser and hoarser without dropping an inch. The everyday man, on the other hand, must do his work, though he is as hoarse as a crow; and when she is practising the new roll his wife ought to be upstairs sewing neatly. It must be easy again for a countess to set apart a room for rolling in, and her husband in the gun-room be never the wiser. In a small house, however, there are no such spare rooms. Consider the distress of a newly married man when he comes home from his honeymoon (which he has had to take alone) and finds his wife rolling in her wedding-dress. For the good of the middle-class public, therefore, you might persuade your brats to set an example in economy. Insist on their having one frock for rolling in, some garment into which they can simply leap. The Countess, I notice, often changes to suit her passions, red velvet being the most popular for Revenge, and corded silk slightly open at the throat for Broken Heart; but our daughters must roll at some cheaper figure.

Yet let us end on a happier note. Your heroines are not only delightful company but prove that the ripe young matrons of Mayfair are more robust than the Harley Street specialists approve. I question if there are many charmers of the middle class who could roll in such pretty disorder without feeling the strain."

In short, Mr. Anon, that man of secret sorrows, found it useless to love, because, after a look at the length and breadth of him, none would listen. Unable to get a hearing in person, which is probably the more satisfactory way when feasible, he discussed the tender passion with them, as you might say, by deputy or in a mask; in other words, he wrote many articles on the subject of love and the passions that purported to come from perturbed undergraduates or haughty lieutenants, by whom women readers, assuming them to be of the proper dimension, were variously stirred. These young gentlemen wrote, as authorities, of what love should be and in the case of women was not; so that they roused many indignant damsels to the frenzy of reply. Mr. Anon had the elation of feeling that Woman listened to him at last, if only at second hand, and that at second hand he may even have made her roll. Like two or three other articles here this appeared in the 'Speaker,' edited by Wemyss Reid, which is chiefly remembered now, I suppose, by the early writings of 'Q.'

CHAPTER XX

"A LOVE-LETTER"—THE COW-WOMAN

I am the lovely aunt (quite lovely) of Tommy aged seven and May aged six, and for the last hour I have been sitting in an open-air arbour trying to write a letter to a warrior. He has demanded of me to say Yes or No, and I do hate being flurried. On top of the arbour Tommy and May sprawl, unseen, save for an occasional leg whose knee is bandaged (May's) or lately let loose (Tommy's), and they are unaware that their talk comes between me and my effort for the army. Around us is a wild garden of golden broom.

'I know who Auntie is writing a letter to,' says Tommy.

'So do I know,' says May. (Possibly she does know.)

'No, you don't.' (He certainly does not.)

'Yes, I do.'

'If you knew who it was you would say.'

'So would you.'

'No, I wouldn't, by jingo.'

'You are using bad words, Tommy.'

215

'Jingo is not a swear; it is what Captain Abinger says.' (Captain Abinger says worse than that; I had better say No to him.)

'Auntie wouldn't say it.' (Well, she wouldn't have done so three months ago, before she knew Captain Abinger.)

'It is men that say it, not muffy ladies.'

'Auntie is not a muffy lady.' (Darling May.)

'If you don't say she is muffy I won't sit with you.'

'She is rather muffy.' (Oh, May.)

'Bill knows who Auntie is writing to, but I'm not going to tell.' (So he got it from Bill the coachman.)

'Neither am I.'

'Because you don't know.'

'Yes, I do.'

'You needn't think I am going to tell you.'

After a pause.

'She is writing a letter to her husband,' says Tommy.

'Auntie isn't, for she is not married, and if she is not married she can't have a husband.' (How girls do pick up the important things.)

'Yes, she can. That is all you know. Auntie has a ring on her finger, and that shows she is married.'

'No, it doesn't, Tommy.'

'Shut up with your Tommy. Bill says only mollycoddles are called Tommy. If you don't call me Thomas I shall go away.'

At this awful threat May nearly falls through the roof. 'Thomas, then. But Auntie is not married.'

'Yes, she is. Did you not see the ring?'

'That doesn't mean she is married. Boys don't know about these things.' (How true. And besides, though I do happen to have a ring, the question at present gnawing my vitals is whether I should enclose it in my letter or keep it for aye. Be quiet, you imps, and let a woman think.)

'Don't they!' exclaims Thomas. 'Why, if it wasn't that men offered to marry them, ladies wouldn't never be married at all. Ladies can't offer to marry men. Bill told me.'

'Auntie's not married.'

'She couldn't have a ring if she wasn't, stupid. Bill says if you throw away the ring, then you are not married any more; and when Bill's wife gets cheeky he takes it off her finger and pretends to throw it away so as to frighten her.' (That horrid Bill; and I had always thought him so superior.)

'Auntie has four rings.'

'I know that. It means she has been married four times.'

'No, it doesn't, Thomas. The old lady that spoke to us in the boat had a heap more rings than four on her fingers.'

'Yes, because she had a heap of husbands. They are called widowers.'

'I know what Auntie is,' says May, triumphant. 'She is not married; she is engaged.'

Tommy's legs kicked, which told me that he was thinking.

'It was engaged I said,' was the result of his thoughts. 'The four rings means she has been engaged four times.'

'Oh, Tommy!' The abandoned little May uttered it with rapture.

'I only said married so as to trick you,' continued Tommy. 'But it is all the same, engaged or married.'

'No, it's not the same.'

After further reflection Tommy retorts, 'Who said it was the same?'

'You did, Tommy—Thomas.'

'It was you said it.'

'How could it be the same thing when it is not?'

'I know what the difference is.'

'So do I.'

'But I'm not going to tell.'

'Neither am I going to tell, Thomas.'

'If you knew you would say it.'

'Auntie told me herself.' (Such a whopper.)

'If you tell me, I'll tell you.'

'Well, then, you are engaged first and then you are married after.'

'That is what I said, May. And you are engaged as long as the man likes.'

'No, as long as the woman likes.' (Dear May.)

'That is all you know, May. The man gives the lady the ring to be engaged with, and then if she is good he marries her, but if she isn't good he takes it back.'

'If he is not good, it is she won't marry him.'

'Yes, she must, May. Ladies only get married if they are good; but men get married whether they are good or not.' He kicked triumphantly.

'That is not fair,' says May in the voice of one who nevertheless feels that Tommy may know.

'Yes, it is. Ladies don't have nothing to do but be good; but men need to be only middling good. Men can say swears sometimes, but not ladies.'

'Papa never says them.'

'Oho: he did yesterday when the door hit his face. He said——'

'I don't want to hear. Was it awful?'

'I told Bill, and he said it was a good one.'

'I know the gentleman Auntie is engaged to,'

says May, probably feeling that she is not scoring.

'So do I.'

'Who is it, then?'

'Look here, May, if you tell me I'll give you my football.'

'But it is lost.'

'Well, I'll give it to you if we find it. Come on, who is Auntie engaged to?'

'It is Captain Abinger.'

'Get out!'

'Honest Injin. He is very nice.'

'He is awfully decent. But engaged to Auntie! I say, does he know?'

''Course he knows, and he likes it.' (If they would only dry up and let me think whether I like it.)

'Will she be his auntie when they are married?'

'No, she will be his wedding wife; but just think, Tommy, he will be our uncle!'

'Lumme!'

'I am to be a bridesmaid, Tommy. (First I have heard of this.)

'So am I.'

'No, you are to be a bridesman.'

'I'm not. They needn't think it.'

'It's very important.' (Not half so important as whether there is to be a bride.)

'What does a bridesman do?' Tommy asks
guardedly.

'He holds up the train.'

'Oh, well, I'll be a bridesman.' (For a
moment I am gratified, but then I remember
that he has lately been told the story of a train-
robber who did that.)

'Tommy.'

'Stow that.'

'Thomas.'

'Well?'

'Do you know what he calls Auntie in his
letters?'

'I know, but I have forgotten.'

'If you say you know I won't tell you.'

'Well, I don't know.'

'Come closer and I'll whisper.' (I suppose
she does whisper, for screams of distasteful mirth
follow.)

'Oh, gee!' cries Tommy.

'Tommy, please, please, don't tell Bill.'

'Rather not.' (They are insufferable. I decide
to write my letter in the house. But what should
I say? Yes or No? What did I intend to say
if these wretches had not confused me?)

'By jingo, May, what an awful sell to Auntie
if he took it back.'

'What?'

'The ring. And I say——' (I collect my
writing things. Through the golden broom I
fly.)"

I REMEMBER Anon's writing this; indeed it was
one of a series (all the others lost), written on a
house-boat which his friend Gilmour and he had
hired for a month or more at Molesey.

I revisited the scene lately and found it was
now as grand as if it were being presented nightly
at Drury Lane. There remained no houseboats
of our humble kind; magnificent successors en-
circled Tagg's Island. Each seems to have a
garden; there is a gorgeous hotel, and there are
putting-greens and lawn-tennis courts and danc-
ing galore. I was discomfited, because I had
thought it a gay place in my day and that I had
been seeing life. Now I know that by comparison
we were all humdrum folk, living prosaically
round a field with a cow on it, a cow that became
the one companion of Anon. There was a little
inn with a bar where he sometimes went forlornly
to listen to the swashbucklers from the other
houseboats. Mr. Anon thought that any one in
flannels was a swashbuckler. I wonder what he

drank at that bar. I think by this time he must have been on the verge of beer. The reason he listened to them was because they often talked about him. A number of articles were appearing in the 'St. James's' about the island (Anon had struck a lucky vein), the island by day, the island by night, life on houseboats, the ferry, the bar-room, the cow, the field, there was even one on 'the pretty girl,' implying that she was not only pretty but that she was the only one. This was the article that gave rise to most discussion at the bar, the question in debate being which of the houseboats had the distinction of harbouring the girl. From her they would be led to wondering who was the author, and fix momentarily on this person or that, sometimes on one of themselves who did not always deny the charge. As for the real author, no one ever suspected him; even on such a little island Mr. Anon failed to impress. As for knowing a pretty girl when he saw one nobody conceived it of the object in the corner. It was equally inconceivable to the ladies of the island, who were chiefly interested in which of them was the pretty girl. I suppose they would have hurled him into the water (as the reader may be inclined to do also) had he up and told them that the pretty girl was really the cow.

This was not cynicism, though it may have

been touched with the pique of the 'quite harm-less.' At some still earlier age, battered by the neglect of the sex, Anon had conceived an esteem for the cow, the placid divinity who chews the cud of life equably, ever the same, yesterday, to-day and to-morrow, judging man more by the way he offers her grass than by his personal attractions. On the island in the heat of the day Anon and the cow often had the field to them-selves, for the flannelled ones were at their offices in the city, and we are speaking of an age when woman did not want to bask and be brown. The cow browsed, and Anon meditated, building up a pretty girl for himself who did not mind a man's being harmless. Thus it was inevitable that she should have many of the adorable qualities of cows. A tinkle of sweet laughter from the houseboats, a flash of picture hats, would remind him of qualities in which cows are as yet deficient, and he would add touches from those ladies who regarded him not; here the soft voice that was awaiting the return of the flannels, there a pair of eyes, blue or green, but bovine. She was always elegant was Anon's pretty girl, but, in justice to the cow, of an attractively indolent carriage and slightly inclined to embonpoint. This kept the interest of the ladies at fever heat, several recognizing themselves for a moment, only to be dumbfounded the next. As for Anon, he never told his love.

In an old note-book I find some entries showing that I once planned a play to the glory of our island cow. The only male character mentioned in the notes is an author whom ladies consider quite harmless. He becomes guardian to a baby-girl and decides to bring her up as a child of nature. The title was to be 'The Cow-Woman,' but the play was never written. Perhaps poor Anon had come to the conclusion that cow-women are the most disturbing of them all.

Farewell, ladies (though I daresay you will crop up again).

If only I could write something harmful.

CHAPTER XXI

"EVEN before we were engaged I kncw of Charles's delicious literary ambition. I was so proud of it. He meant to write a play, not an ordinary play, but the one for which everybody who knows the great plays of the past has been calling for years. We felt a little self-conscious when we heard those demands for a real play, and even nervous lest some one should write it before Charles had settled the preliminaries. I was the chief preliminary, but there were others connected with business, for by day he is only a clerk, though a much valued one, and has to give to the ledger many hours that really ought to be at the service of the public.

I sometimes sighed over this, because it prevented his beginning at once to write the darling play; but he was undaunted. 'You will find,' he said cheerily, 'that the big artistic things have nearly always been done by men who seemed to have no spare time in which to do them. Obstacles

226

were made merely to be overcome.   I am firmly
convinced that what is in a man will out.'

As soon as summer arrived he was to begin.

One of his first presents to me was the works
of Aristotle, a famous Greek author (385–
322 B.C.) who knew exactly how a perfect play
should be written.   I was very angry with the
dramatic critic of the 'Times' for constantly
calling attention to this writer, lest, as I have
said, some other dramatist might read him and
write Charles's play.

Charles glowed with quiet fire when he spoke
to me of the play, and he told me a number of
things about it, quite the most delightful of which
was that he would never really have understood
women if he had not known me.   'There are
to be little bits of the heroine,' he would say,
'which will be simply chipped off you.'   Often
of an evening before our marriage when he and
I sat together I could not raise my eyes to his
because I had the exquisite sensation that he was
chipping.

Our engagement was not of long duration, for
Charles coaxed me to church in these words,
'Time is on the wing, and I cannot settle down
to the play until we are married.'

We built our sweet new furniture, as one may
say, round the play, giving it one entire room,

with everything there that we felt it could possibly want, and so we had to be comparatively skimpy in the furnishing of the other rooms. I don't know which of us was the more anxious to make sacrifices for the sake of the play; the same thought often leapt to both minds at once, 'Yes, truly that drawing-room settee is a dream, but let us rather buy that study table with the secret drawer; it will so help me (you) at your (my) work, and once the play is launched we can have a surfeit of settees.' Our taste was too fine to want a surfeit of them, but I did want one settee.

'Every evening,' I told him, 'you will find your manuscript (we pronounced it MS.—I do so love that word) lying on the table waiting for you. But you must not work too hard at it,' I insisted; 'you must have fixed hours, and at a certain time, say at ten o'clock, I shall simply order you to cease writing for the night.'

He saw the wisdom of this, but at the same time shook his head over its practicability. 'You don't know,' he said (he was always a great reader, and indeed has a book-plate), 'how the hours rush by on wings when one is in the throes of inspiration. I shall often feel when ten strikes that I have just begun.'

I vowed that I would come behind him at ten

and softly snatch the pen from his hand, as if I was a darling Dora.

'Every Saturday evening,' he promised, 'I shall read to you what I have written during the week.'

We were married on a September day (15th), and quite an appreciable part of the honeymoon was spent in talk about the play and its heroine. I got him to promise to make her a brunette in case she was so like me as to raise smiles among our friends. Often from the movement of his fingers I knew, while we sat in evening-dress in the exquisite lounge of our hotel, that he was yearning to be writing the play, and nothing proved the depth of his affection more than his not yielding to the temptation. I often told him so, and he admitted it laughingly, saying that I read him like a play.

Conceive us at home in our dear little house at Willesden. 'Will you begin the very first evening?' I asked him as soon as we had run up and down the stairs a few times and peeped sharply into all the rooms as if to take the pets by surprise. His wish was to do so, but he felt it would be wiser to settle down first. 'I shall keep off it for a week,' he said firmly.

'Please, not for my sake,' I begged him, for I had watched his hungry look at the study table.

'For your sake entirely,' he said in his dear way.

'But isn't it a pity to waste any more time?'

He did just a little surprise me.

'There is no such violent hurry,' he said rather testily: it was the first time I had ever heard that note in his voice except when speaking to a cabman, and we don't speak to them often. I suppose he noticed my surprise (he notices everything), for he added, 'The time won't be wasted, I can be thinking.'

'But you have thought so long,' I said.

This was silly of me. 'Isn't the lack of thought,' he reminded me, pulling my ears, 'acknowledged to be the curse of the drama?'

We had of course a good many callers at this time, and rather imprudently I told them about the play. They were so interested, and continued to be so interested, that I afterwards regretted it. When the week had become a fortnight I insisted on leaving Charles alone in the study after dinner. He looked rather gloomy, but I filled the ink-bottles (one for red ink because he likes his MS. to be so neat) and put the dreadfully large sheets of paper before him. As my share of the work (this had been planned during the honeymoon) I wrote the title of the play, which had been fixed on long before (and a most

tantalizing title it is), though I was sworn to
secrecy, because if divulged it might be stolen
(such is the state of the copyright laws). I also
wrote the words 'Act I,' and kissed the place
beneath them, also a tiny blank spot on the back
of Charles's head, and handed him the pen. He
did not, however, thank me. I don't mean that
he was unkind, he is never that, but he certainly
did not thank me.

An hour afterwards I slipped into the study
with a cup of tea for him. He was sitting by
the fire with the cat on his knee and an odd
expression on his face, as if the cat were his only
friend.

'You were not sleeping, Charles?' I asked
before I saw the cat.

'Sleeping,' he said rather indignantly, as if I
had charged him with some crime. 'No, I am
thinking.'

'Again,' I said thoughtlessly.

He asked me almost tartly what I meant by
'again.'

I said I only meant that he had not written
anything yet.

'I was just going to begin when you came in,'
he said; 'I shall begin as soon as I have drunk
this tea.'

But when I returned at ten to insist on his

stopping work he was still nursing the cat. I didn't like to look at the MS.

Next evening Charles said he felt a curious disinclination for writing, and thought he would take a night off. I must have looked disappointed, for though he is the gentlest of men he flared up.

'I can't be eternally writing,' he growled; but fortunately I like his growling.

'But you haven't done anything at all yet.'

Of course this was inconsiderate of me, and I think he took it rather nicely. All he said was, 'Don't you think that is a rather ungenerous way of putting it?' I reminded him, 'But you always spoke as if the work would be such a pleasure to you.'

'Have I said, my dear, that it is not a pleasure? If you knew anything of literary history you would know that there are times when the most industrious writers cannot pen a line. My present feeling is merely a proof that I have the artistic temperament, and surely it is all to the good to find that I have that.'

'Still,' I said diffidently, 'they must all make a beginning some time.'

'Undoubtedly,' he said, 'and I shall make mine to-morrow.'

To-morrow came, however, without finding him in the study. He almost implored me to let him spend the evening hanging the bedroom pictures.

I said I could not possibly drag him away from the play.

'You are in a most uncommon desperate hurry to see me shut myself up with that play,' he said; it was the first time he had called it 'that play.'

'You spoke as if you were so anxious to begin it.'

'So I am; have I said I was not?'

He marched off to the study, banging the drawing-room door, but I do love him when he bangs. An hour or so afterwards I again took him tea, and somehow I knew that between his hearing the rattle of the cup and saucer and the opening of the door he had sprung from the couch to the study table, where I found him pen in hand. I noticed also that one arm was raised as a barricade against my seeing the MS.

'How are you getting on?' I said nevertheless out of sheer niceness, and this time he had the effrontery to reply, 'Excellently, oh excellently.' And yet except on this one matter I suppose there never was a more truthful man.

He drank his tea so slowly that it could only have been because he was reluctant to reach the bottom of the cup. I tried to look over the barricade, but it at once rose higher.

'I shall come in to stop you at ten sharp,' I said, preparing to go.

He tried to be appealing and brazen at the same time.

'I think I have perhaps done enough for one night,' he said, 'I mustn't overdo it.'

'But how much have you done?'

He made an evasive reply about quality being better than quantity, and muttered something about writer's cramp.

'If you would like me to be your amanuensis——' I began, but he would not hear of that. He declined to make a slave of his wife.

'Do read me the opening scene,' I begged him, but he preferred that I should wait till Saturday. When Saturday came he was not in the mood for reading it. He was not even in the mood for writing it; he was in the mood for mending the kitchen clock. He became quite a handy man about the house, except in the study.

So the play-writing went on.

One morning when he was at the office I counted the clean sheets (the first page was missing), and found they were just as I had placed them on the table the evening before. He had not even torn any of them up that night. Thus it went on for a week or two, with this difference: he either suspected that I peeped in

his absence or thought I might take it into my
head to do so. He therefore now locked away
the MS. (as we still called it) in a drawer. I had
a key which could unlock that drawer, and here
is a really lovely little story about me, complete
in one sentence, I never did unlock the drawer,
no, not even when I accidentally discovered that
he added several clean pages nightly to those left
on the desk in order to deceive me about the
progress of the work. His new way of avoiding
Saturday was to say that it would be better not
to read any of the play aloud to me until a whole
act was finished.

Then the study became, I suppose, so detest-
able to him that he had to take stronger action.
He came home one day from the city with a pair
of spectacles. 'Yes, it does seem a pity,' he
admitted, when I shrank from the horrid things,
'but I must take care of my eyesight, and what
with all this writing by such poor gas light——'
Here he paused to let me say something; I knew
so well by this time what he wanted me to say,
and I am such a good wife, that I gulped and
said it. The upshot was a decision to postpone
any further work on the play, or to defer beginning the play (I forget how we put it), until the
long days set in. May was the month I suggested
for resumption, but he insisted on April. April

arrived (the middle of it), and I said I thought it would be a good omen if he resumed work on the 23rd, which was the birthday of another dramatist (1564–1616).

'You are eternally talking about that play,' he snapped, which was almost unkind of him, for the play was the one subject now tabooed in our little home by unspoken mutual agreement.

'Because you used to be so enthusiastic about it,' I said.

'I am as enthusiastic as ever, but I can't be always writing the thing.' He said 'thing.'

'We have now been married seven months and you haven't shown me a line yet,' I said.

He retired to the study in dudgeon and sat staring at the MS. as I daresay a hen may regard an egg that isn't there. My chief feeling about Charles is usually pride, but I felt very sorry for him that night when he broke down and told me everything. His play has a splendid plot, with delightful scenes and some of the darlingest touches of character (especially in the heroine). It is absolutely the play for which every one has been calling. This I knew from the first, for he had again and again regaled me with titbits on our honeymoon. What, then, was the trouble? It was this; Charles simply could not find a beginning for his play. All the rest he knew, but he could not begin.

It had been very noble of him to try to save me pain by keeping this wretched little trouble from me for so long, and I hope I was a loving wife to him that evening.

'It does seem tragic,' I said, 'that such a small thing should stand between us and fame, and my advice is that you abandon the project altogether. After all, the country has the plays it deserves.'

Charles is so tenacious, however, that this proposal brought no comfort to him, and he insisted on continuing the struggle—but not that evening.

'You are so dogged,' I said.

'I suppose I am too dogged,' he admitted, 'but I can't change my nature.'

I was in his confidence now, and he let me try to think out a beginning. I thought of a lovely one: the curtain to rise on two servants dusting, and telling who the other characters were. But strange to say, I found that this was the only beginning which Charles had thought of himself and that he had abandoned it because he discovered it was the way all the other clerks in the office began their plays. Thus I was no great help, but our thinking of the same beginning is a delightful proof that Charles and I are not twain but one.

That summer it was so pleasant to be out of doors that Charles was little in the study. Sometimes he thought of writing in the orchard, but there was the danger of the MS. being blown away.

The winter was such an unusually hard one that his fingers froze if he sat for any length of time at the study table. We often discussed the advisability of pushing the study table near the fire. But it is too heavy for one, and that winter he was specially anxious that I should not over-exert myself. So many exquisite evenings we had that winter, crouching over the blazing logs; nothing between us and bliss except that hateful MS.

For ever and ever and ever was the date to which I now wanted Charles to abandon the work, but he still clung to the idea of resumption at some future time.

'Let us say this day one year hence,' I suggested.

He thought that was too definite.

'Well, then, let us say till an idea strikes you.'

He had some objection to that also; I forget now what it was. We finally decided that he should cease the actual writing of the play 'until he had had time to look round.' I don't know why, but this phrase pleased him very much.

Never since that happy day has the MS. given us the slightest trouble. The phrase, on the other hand, has been changed several times. It has been 'until we move into a more convenient house,' and 'until we have settled down in the new house,' and at present it is 'until the children are older.' You must not think that Charles has given up the idea of being a dramatist; I have never known him fuller of it than during the last year or two. I notice also that he now speaks of the project cheerily to our friends, which by-the-by I have ceased to do.

We are now nearly middle-aged, and I love Charles more than ever, perhaps just because I know him better. I also love his little MS. Never again shall I speak slightingly of it. It has been a success to me. Our enormous interest in it was what first brought us together; perhaps but for it our glorious union would never have had a beginning. So you see Charles began *my* play beautifully though he may not be able to begin his own (but that remains to be seen)."

THUS do the Gods mock their might-have-beens. This luckless Charles probably never found a beginning for his play, and so far as I can discover not one page exists of his virgin MS. Gone similarly into the waste are nearly all the many hundred MSS. of Anon's articles, this of 'My Husband's Play' being (for some great end unknown to me) among the few exceptions. In his day if there was such a thing as typewriting he had never heard of it; all the articles he sent to the 'St. James's' and elsewhere were in this same shaky scrawl, and oh, it is ill to read. I suppose there were other contributors who wrote no better, and I marvel how Greenwood found time to decipher us and yet edit his paper. It has taken me half an hour to stumble through this article, and even then I leapt some of the words. How much more fortunate the editors of to-day with their demand for typing.

In my schooldays I wrote the most boastful copperplate; sometimes of an evening I still gaze at it with proud bewilderment. It went, I think, not gradually with over-writing, but suddenly like my smile. If the two ever meet in whatever Valhalla such things go to when they leave us, one would like to think that they quaff a goblet to Anon.

About fifteen years ago a great change for the better came over my handwriting. Even proofreaders, so cunning at their job, had at times

asked me to translate, but I was saved by an
attack of writer's cramp to which, once abhorred,
I now make a reverential bow, though it is as
ready as ever to pounce if thoughtlessly I take
up the pen in my right hand. I had to learn
to write with the left, not so irksome to me as
it would be to most, for I am naturally left-handed
(and still kick with the left foot). I had never
from infancy written with the left hand, however,
and progress was slow. I now write as easily
with this hand as once with the other, and if I
take any pains the result is almost pleasing to
the eye. The hope of my friends is that I shall
never recover my facility with the other. Nevertheless, there is not the same joy in writing with
the left hand as with the right. One thinks
down the right arm, while the left is at best an
amanuensis. The right has the happier nature,
the left is naturally sinister. I write things with
the left, or to put the matter I think more correctly, it writes things with me, that the right
would have expressed more humanely. I never,
so far as I can remember, wrote uncomfortable
tales like 'Dear Brutus' and 'Mary Rose' till I
crossed over to my other hand. I could not have
written these, as they are, with my right hand
any more than I could have written 'Quality
Street' with my left. Anon of course was right-

handed. If he had written this little sketch 'My Husband's Play' with the left it would probably have ended quite differently, say with the wife leaving her husband in disdain, or even writing his play herself.

CHAPTER XXII

"THE CLUB GHOST"—WHAT DOES ONE DO IN CLUBS?—HENRY JAMES—THE ADELPHI BY NIGHT

"The club library is a pleasantly gloomy room overlooking St. James's Street, and its walls are reported by some to be lined with books. Others, however, think they are only dummies, and as glass doors separate them from members, no one will perhaps ever know for certain.

Though I have been a member of the club for a year I do not even now know a soul in the ancient place. If any other member were to address me, so surely have I fallen into the club ways that I should probably complain to the committee, and I presume he would behave similarly if I addressed him. I, who was once sociable, go from door to door in the club looking for a room in which I can be alone. When I find it I either sit motionless in the window or slumber by the fire, vaguely conscious that other members, also seeking clubable facilities, have, now and again, peeped in and finding me in

possession have departed petulantly. It is the
cosiest club in London, but I am still young,
and after my disturbing experience of to-day
I contemplate removing my name from the
books.

I woke, dimly conscious that I was in the
library and that the servants must have forgotten
to light the gas. Perhaps I shifted my position
a little, for an ash-tray fell off the arm of my
chair. I did not know for certain (I now speak
as one giving evidence in a Court of Law) that
it was an ash-tray. I will not swear on oath that
it was an ash-tray. I believe it was an ash-tray.
I swear, however, that I heard something fall,
and immediately a voice growled 'Sh-sh.' I paid
no attention, but presently I remembered that of
course when I fell asleep I was alone in the room.
Had I heard 'Sh-sh'? The fire gleamed for a
moment, but I opened my eyes too late. I was
almost slumbering in a sleeping again, but not
quite, for I could hear myself breathing heavily.
Then it struck me that what I heard was not my
own breathing. Evidently the intruder was in
the chair by the window. The fire brightened,
and I looked at the chair drowsily. There was
no one there. I looked at the other chairs. They
were empty. Still I heard heavy breathing, followed by a yawn as if the man was stretching

himself. I yawned myself, and my yawn was an echo of his. Or was his an echo of mine? They were strangely similar. Who was he, and how did he get into the room without my knowledge? But, stop—where was he? I fixed my eyes, now wide open, on the chair by the window, from which those sounds seemed to proceed. The room was again in dusk. I stretched out my foot gently to where his legs ought to have been, but it encountered nothing. I drew my foot back in some surprise, and, leaning forward, felt for him with my hands. They slid down an arm of the chair, and then into space. Had I not been a club-man I would have risen in agitation. Evidently the fellow was awake, wherever he had bestowed his limbs, and I made no scruple, therefore, of for the first time addressing a fellow-member. 'Very careless of these servants,' I began, 'not lighting the——' 'Sh-sh,' came the one familiar club sound. I patted the floor with my foot in the sternest manner, but of course he was within his rights. Then a coal poised improperly on the fire by the library attendant toppled from the grate, with the result that a flicker of flame sprang up. Now I saw him plainly. He was a dog, a grey Skye terrier, looking as old as Skye. It was not his being a dog so much as the very old look that gave me the sinking. I remembered that there was an uncomfortable story about our club, something about shadowy figures on the stair. At the moment, however, emotion of any kind would have been out of place in that room. I twisted myself more comfortably in my chair, for I know the way of being comfortable in our library chairs, however agitated one may be, and when I had done so I caught sight of myself in the mirror. What I saw made me again turn to the dog; this time almost sharply. He was lying in his chair exactly as I lay in mine. Probably I looked at him uneasily now, and then I looked once more in the glass. What a bored face I had; where had I seen such a face recently? I started; I believe I glared at the dog, for an unpleasant suspicion had crossed my mind. Yes, the dreariness of his expression was horribly like mine. He glanced across and scowled as if annoyed because I had intruded on his privacy. 'Well?' I said, with affected jocularity, yet cautiously, for I always wonder what a dog will do next. He looked me up and down, and then calmly turned his back on me. 'On my word,' I began, when he whisked round, and again I heard that club 'Sh-sh.'

From this point I have to confess that I was overstrung, and would have been glad to escape from the room. I suppose I was afraid to move, as I continued to lie back in my chair. My companion was still lolling in his. To assert my manhood I was on the point of coolly trimming my nails, a club privilege, when I heard a scraping, and desisted on seeing that he was doing what I had been about to do. At last he rose, and muttering languidly to himself cautiously stepped on to the floor as one does in clubs. I held my breath when I saw him strolling to the bell. Perhaps he changed his mind, for instead of ringing he yawned again, cast a careless glance at the mirror as if he were wearing a necktie, and with a frown at me walked limply to the door. He left it ajar—his first incorrect action. I bounced after him—mine.

He descended the stairs stolidly, as we all do, looking neither to right nor left; the bored expression still on his face. I leant over the banisters to see the last of him. He cast an eye on an evening newspaper framed in the hall, but did not read it (none of us do), and paused near the hall-porter as if to ask if there were any letters. Then he stepped prosily to the entrance door. The page-boys, who were of great age, opened it for him, and he courteously inclined his head without regarding them. I waited to give him time, if such was his wish, to hail a cab.

'What dog was that?' I then asked of the hall-porter.

He would not have told, or indeed have spoken to, any one else, but of course he had to answer a member. The dog had been owned by a member of many years ago, the Rev. James Spens, a power in the club, and it had usually accompanied him on his daily visits thereto. The hall-porter, who spoke as one not certain that I should like it, said he could remember the dog as a bright, merry creature, but that as he got used to the club he changed. This was specially noticeable after they made him a member, which was some time before his master's death.

'A member?' I exclaimed.

An honorary member, the hall-porter interposed hurriedly, apparently hoping that this might mitigate the offence. It seems that on some great occasion of the past the club members lost their sense of propriety for a night and dined together, instead of at separate tables, with the result that the Skye terrier, on the motion of his master (who was in an odd condition), had been elected an honorary member. The intention was humorous, but was not so taken by the dog. Unexpected results followed. The gaiety went out of the new member. He became crusty, snapped at William if the two pages were not

there to throw open the door as he reached the
last step, was condescending though quite the
gentleman to the servants, and life-weary with
members, was very nice about his food and
barked if he thought he was in a draught. 'When
we first knew him just as a dog,' William said
with a slight quiver, 'he was a one to play with
an apple, balancing it on his head, like a music-
hall, but in the days I speak of he would no more
have done tricks with an apple than any other
member of the club.' William never said 'the
club' without nearly crossing himself.

The dog now sometimes came to the club
before his master and would wander its premises
looking for a room devoid of other living orna-
ments; but this, William assured me, was not
done for himself but in the interests of the Rev.
Mr. Spens, for whom he kept the room. His
affection for his master remained to the last the
one unclubable thing about him. On the death
of Mr. Spens he would not enter the club for
weeks, though sometimes seen looking at it in a
daze from across the street. By and by, however,
he resumed his attendance and was now a frequent
visitor. He considered the library to be his
special room, and he had one chair in it between
the fire and the window where he was usually to
be found. Mr. Mannering and Sir George also

liked this chair, and there was such bickering for it among the three of them as William never saw in all his time.

'I don't like it, William,' I said.

'Nobody likes it, sir,' said he, 'but we can't do anything.'

'It seems to me that as he cannot pay his subscription——'

'An honorary member,' William pointed out, 'pays no subscription.'

'Still, after all, he is only a dog.'

'In a way, sir,' William said guardedly.

'But the committee——'

'I understand, sir, that the subject came up before them years and years ago, and that they took legal advice but they had no case; so the counsels decided. They said that some barrister on the make would take the matter up and perhaps drive the club into bankruptcy. We servants,' William went on doubtfully, 'we rather likes the little varmint—the old gentleman as I might say, sir.'

'Has he a name?'

'We call him Mr. Spens, sir—without the "Rev."' William now obviously wished me to go away. It determined me to ask him more, though in a lower voice.

'You are sure he is a living dog, William?'

'He was once, sir,' was all that the loyal
servant of the club would reply.

'Do you ever lift him up——or even touch
him?'

'A member, sir!' he said, outraged.

'Answer my question, William.'

'Not of late years, sir,' he said huskily.

'Why not?'

'He——he snaps, sir.'

'That is not your real reason. Be a man. Is
it because you think he is not there?'

'It might be that, sir.'

'I won't harass you further, William. But
what do you make of it all?'

'It might be,' the old retainer whispered, 'that
he came here too often, sir, in the days when——
when he was a member. Some of the members
drop in so often that——that they don't know
where else to go to . . . after the obsequies,
sir.'

'Are those the shadows on the stair that I have
heard spoken of?' I cried, scared. 'Do you mean
that even the Rev. Mr. Spens——'

'Don't, sir,' William implored.

'You yourself, William,' I could not help
saying, 'though you must be very old, you are
real, aren't you, William?'

'If you please, sir. Thank you, sir,' he said.

I desisted, but I don't like it.
Signed before witnesses."

NEVER, despite this effort of Mr. Anon's, can there have been any one more unlike a club-man than I. I daresay I am the only member of clubs who need not take his warning to heart. I 'belong' nowadays to at least half a dozen of the stately edifices, but I enter none oftener than, say, quinquennially, and the others less frequently. A canine member is not needed to keep me out but to draw me in.

I have no ill-will to clubs; indeed I am still sometimes caught momentarily in the webs they weave across Pall Mall; a club hair touches my face as I am passing, just sufficient to remind me that I am a member here; I ascend the steps, then I remember and hasten away. What I remember is that I could never find out what one does in clubs; I know about hanging up my hat; then you sit down on a chair and cross your legs, but what does one do after he has crossed his legs? Anon went to London thinking that clubs were Romance, wondering if ever the glorious day would come when callers at his 'chambers,' on finding he was out, would know that therefore he must be at 'the club.' He even saw, did Anon (in his mind's eye, O Thackeray), ladies inquiring for him first at those chambers and next with certainty at that club. So he was ripe for Bohemia; clubs even gave him a thrill (which he was never to get from them again) when he joined his first, the Savage. I remember his elation. A kindly acquaintance, already a member thereof, made the terrific announcement that he believed he could get Anon in. He took the trembling one to the headquarters of the club in Adelphi Terrace, put him into a room on the ground floor with padded seats (which made Anon to glow, they were so obviously the real thing), asked him to look more clubable, and then left him alone for a long time, occasionally sending down various friends to look him over and see if he would do. I often pass that way nowadays, being resident in the Latin Quarter, and seem to see Anon on one of the padded seats with his legs crossed while he tries to look club-able. He little thought, poor soul, that he already knew nearly all he and I were ever to know about what one does in clubs.

I have no intention of recounting my various clubs, but the next was the Reform, out of which, so far as frequenting it was concerned, I was

driven by Henry James. I liked him well, but
I had discovered another thing you can do in
clubs, you can get your hair cut there. I naturally
clung to that, but, alas, James, who was a true
frequenter, clung to it also, and when one is
swaddled in that white cloth one wants no friendly
neighbour. At such times he and I conversed
amiably from our chairs with raging breasts.
Then one day I was in Manchester or Liverpool
in a big hotel, and it came to me that now was
my chance to get my hair cut in peace. I went
downstairs, and just as they enveloped me in the
loathly sheet I heard a groan from the adjoining
chair and saw that its occupant was Henry James.
After a moment, when anything might have
happened, we both laughed despairingly, but I
think with a plucky sympathy, meaning that fate
was too much for us. Later in the day we discussed the matter openly for the first time, but
could come to no conclusion for future guidance.
Each, however, without making any promise, did
something to help. Feeling that I had been
driven from society by its greatest ornament I
let my hair go its own wild way, and he, though
he remained in society, removed his beard, which
was what had taken him so often to the salon of
the artists. Not that I can claim the beard as a
trophy of mine, but he did remove it about that

time, and I should have been proud to be the shears, for the result was that at last his full face came into the open, and behold it was fair. One saw at last the lovely smile that had so long lain hidden in the forest.

No man of letters, I suppose, ever had a more disarming smile than his, and smiles, as I have told, are a subject about which I can speak with authority. It was worth losing a train (and sometimes you had to do that) while he rummaged for the right word. During the search the smile was playing about his face, a smile with which he was on such good terms that it was a part of him chuckling at the other parts of him. I remember once meeting him in the street and asking him how he liked a lecture we had both lately attended. I did not specially want to know nor he to tell, and as he sought for the right words it began to rain, and by and by it was raining heavily. In this predicament he signed to a passing growler and we got in and it remained there stationary until he reached the triumphant conclusion, which was that no one could have delivered a lecture with less offence. They certainly were absolutely the right words, but the smile's enjoyment while he searched for them was what I was watching. It brought one down like Leather-stocking's Killdeer.

I never was so intimate with any other club as to have my hair cut in it, but in the after-days when I knew for certain that there was no rule compelling you to go to a club though you were a member, I joined a number. The only one I almost go to, however, is still the Savage, where long ago I so knowingly crossed my legs. I am not even a member of it now, but for the last twenty years I have lived in an eyry so near this club that through my windows I can note the Savages going in and out as if I were in a lofty private box. They look so happy and waft such gaiety on stilly Saturday nights that I am sure there is more to it than crossing your legs. They have such a reputation for being Bohemians that never surely could I have the heart to tell them that the real Bohemia begins in Adelphi Terrace after the last of them has departed for the night. Then from my eyry, as the ghosts come out, I look upon the only club whose ways I really know, the club of the Adelphi ghosts.

Very likely the first ghost to emerge is Davy Garrick, so dapper in his knee-breeches. I call to some of them from my perch, but he has never been sufficiently near because he always comes to his home in the Terrace by Adam Street, and I am at the other end. Mrs. Bracegirdle tells me that there is a large room on the first floor of his house, so crammed with the MSS. of plays that you could never get inside if the door did not open outwards. Once, she says, he had a house-cleaning and threw all the MSS. into the river. I ought to explain that after the Savage is locked up for the night there is no Embankment, no gardens, and, as in the old days, the river has drawn very near. The only time she ever saw Garrick in a rage, Mrs. Bracegirdle says, was next day, when kindly wherrymen brought the bundles of MSS. back to him, very wet and muddy.

I see Dr. Johnson and Mr. Boswell come out of Garrick's house, and the great lexicographer as usual crosses the road to tap the rails and count them. They are not the rails of to-day, but, as old prints show, three times as high. Johnson often gets confused in his counting and has to begin again. Sometimes this irritates me and I open my window and call out '179' or the like, at which he shakes his staff at me and Boswell looks up in amazement at my hardihood. They march away, nearly running into Peter the Great who is gossiping at my corner with Mr. Pepys and one Rousseau. The brothers Adam patrol the Adelphi still in the small hours, ready to hand over to the watch any one who may be presuming to alter their designs, and they would

R

ascend to my eyry to ask who had dared to put it here were it not that they are frightened at the lift. They look with suspicious eye on three revellers, Mr. Micawber, the Fat Boy and Charles Lamb, who have just left Rowlandson's corner and are disturbing by their shouts another ghost at a window across the way, who is Gibbon, very busy correcting the proof-sheets of the 'Decline and Fall.'

Lamb has no qualification to be here. He was never, alas, one of ours, but we who live in the Adelphi were so shamed by not being able to claim him that after a meeting (which took place in the eyry) we went to the Temple in a fog and collared his ghost and brought it along. We had to keep him roped at first (and it is not easy to rope a ghost) because he had heard there was a Scotsman among us, and as he has told us he was convinced that no Scot loved him. Oh, Charles Lamb! Now he has stutteringly apologized for what he once wrote on that subject, and of all my visitors he is the most desired. He delights in the novelty of the lift as much as the Adam brothers detest it, and sometimes he thinks he has called on me when really he has only gone up and down many times in the lift. I never knew any one so sympathetic nor with such a gift for ghostly talk; as when he asks me how

my William is getting on in Australia with the
pretty young wife, and how fares my Dick on
whom the kettle fell, and where that rogue Harry
is, and was it Bob who ran off with Charlotte or
Charlotte with Bob, and about Jane and Emily
and all the rest of that large family he has invented
for me.

Americans, with every virtue except that they
are not ghosts, sometimes call to ask me to tell
them about the historical interests of the Adelphi,
and I find they are less agape for word of those
who have lived here than for others who have
never lived at all but seem nevertheless to be
more alive. These are chiefly people in Dickens's
magic glass, such as David Copperfield, who went
to a party given by Steerforth round the corner
and was sure somebody was drunk and found in
time that it was himself. As I can only show the
spot by going on my roof, I am afraid I occasionally show one of my own rooms instead. Some
of the inquirers have also gone away under the
impression subtly conveyed that it was in the
eyry that the maid threw the water on Walter
Raleigh, another of our ghosts, when she first
saw smoke issuing from his mouth. The real
disturbing maid of the Adelphi, however, is
Emma Hart, better known as Lady Hamilton.
As her ghost strolls the Terrace after Savages

are far away in bed she is still just Emma Hart, chambermaid to a famous quack-doctor in the Terrace. I watch her of a moonlit night, posing divinely against area rails, as if she thought some lurking artist might be already painting her. (O luckless I, who craved in my youth to be a painter, and only gave up the calling because I always lost my paints.) She strolls along, twinkling as she passes the darkened club, being amused, I suppose, because the members think they are Bohemians.

I gather from the public prints that our Latin Quarter is now 'ripe for development,' which may mean that we are ripe for the development which Garrick gave to the poor MSS. When next I meet the Savages it may be in the water —Bohemians at last. There will be a ghost on the back of every one of us, and I shall try to get Charles Lamb.

CHAPTER XXIII

" ANON AND I "

"YESTERDAY Mr. Anon produced his first play, and being interested in the fellow I bought the news-sheets this morning to see what they thought of it and him. They agreed that it was among the most hopeless things ever offered to our kind friends in front, and though I was sorry for poor Anon I felt that I should like to see how he took his castigation. So I put the newspapers in my pocket, and set off, as one might say, to call on him. I found the doomed wretch in Grenville Street smoking a cigar which was constantly going out.

'Seen the papers?' I asked pleasantly.

'And you also, Brutus!' he said, or words to that effect; 'considering our relationship I think you should be the last to rub it in.'

'For your good, Anon,' I said, though not so very harshly. I looked around at the familiar room. 'After all you seem to have breakfasted well,' I added.

He shrugged, with an indifference that ill became him.

'It was not always so in Grenville Street,' I

reminded him; 'nor once upon a time were there cigars, O Anon.'

'I am not complaining,' he retorted, and tried to light the cigar again. It was difficult to know what consolation to give him, but I did my best.

'I think it plucky of you,' I said, 'to take it so calmly. I daresay if I had been slated in that way I should never have been able to hold up my head. Let me light your cigar for you; your hand seems a little shaky this morning.'

'I notice the same about yours,' he said, with a funereal laugh.

'I cannot remember any play's getting such a slating,' I assured him thoughtfully, though with some exaggeration. 'You saw what one paper said about pathos and bathos? Severe certainly, but uncommonly clever. Finlayson and I were much amused by another critic on your ideas of comedy; indeed I think Finlayson is putting the cutting into his scrap-book. How did you feel when you read Jenison? After all, he let you off more lightly than Bertram. If you did not see Bertram on your sense of humour I have it with me.'

'I have seen them all,' Anon replied, spilling a boxful of vestas and looking at me reproachfully. Just then we heard a boy shouting the glad news that the evening papers were upon the town.

'I 'll go out and bring them in,' I said.

'Don't trouble yourself,' he answered. I insisted that it was no trouble, and went out for the papers. I gave him two of them, and read aloud titbits from the others.

'Well, what does the "Nettle" say?' I asked as I saw him crumple up the paper. The crumpling was his sufficient reply.

'Whatever it says,' I continued, 'you will find its bludgeoning to be almost balm after the persiflage of the "St. James's."'

'The "St. James's!"' he echoed scornfully. He really said that loved word scornfully, did James Anon.

'Here,' I said, frowning, 'is something more palatable. It says the acting was worthy of a better play. That is comforting. Ah, and here is a friend in need who says he saw a more banal piece in the year '82. That is not so long ago.'

'Well,' said Anon, 'I know the worst now.'

'I question that,' I said, clapping him on the back. 'We have not seen the weekly papers yet, and they are sure to be down on you for those historical inaccuracies.'

Anon, I was pleased to see, tried to swagger, but he was white of face. There was also, I doubt not, a craven whiteness on my own.

'I cannot remember another case (nor can Finlayson),' I said doggedly, 'in which the Ibsenite critics and the anti-Ibsenites were so entirely agreed. I should not wonder, young sir, though your play has done some good after all.'

'In what way, you brute?'

'Well, it shows that those who plumb the intellectual depths do have points in common. The public were beginning to think that the one set of critics praised everything conventional, and the other set everything unconventional; but all are agreed as to your piece. I believe you have cleared the ether, Anon.'

'I am glad my play has proved of service if only in that way,' he answered stiffly.

'How luxurious,' I pointed out, 'to be bitter in the first floor front instead of in the cell at the end of the passage. And I am not at all sure, O friend of my youth,' I continued warmly, 'that this wholesale condemnation is not a better tonic than half-hearted praise. Had alluring things been found in the play some manager might have put it into his evening bill, and had to descend with it to Avernus. Also, you might have been tempted to go on writing dramatic dirges and reading them to your writhing friends. Who knows, Anon, but that, in saving you from this, the enemy may have done the state some service?'

'Is it yourself you are trying to buoy up or me?' inquired the shrewd creature.

'I observe,' I admitted handsomely, 'that we occupy the same ditch.'

'Do you agree with their verdict?' he asked me presently.

He spoke so wistfully that, remembering what he had been to me, I was loath to deliver the blow. However, if we were to be of any further use to each other it had to be done.

'On consideration, do you?' I asked. 'Come on, Anon, you of the cigar and the first floor; don't be an ungrateful ass.'

'There is a certain pleasure in grousing,' he said with Scottish dourness.

'But no profit,' said I with Scottish canniness.

Neither of us can smile, but after a struggle he jerked on to his face a look that I understood, because it is the best I can do myself.

'Heigho,' we said simultaneously, and then we sauntered forth with pallid cheeriness to Soho and had luncheon for one."

THE play was the already mentioned 'Richard Savage,' and the stubborn cheeriness of the article brought me a well-wisher among the critics, A. B. Walkley of the 'Times.' His support in after years was what made me go on writing plays. With him, William Archer of blessed memory, who did as much I think for the drama of his time as Pinero himself or, later, G. B. S., whom I used to see in those old days tearing along the Strand with his coat-tails in pursuit of him, and wondered who he was, he was so unlike all other men. His coat-tails pursue him still, but they will never make up on him; no one will ever make up on him. In time I mesmerized Walkley so that he found good in even my poorest efforts, and if he did have to jump on me I felt that his artistic joy in it as a pastime was gone. He and Archer (though Archer sighed over me more than he commended) were the two who made me do my little best in a walk of literature that I at first trod rather contemptuously. I am pleased to know of myself that I was not one who tossed unfavourable criticisms aside, I took my revenge instead in considering them carefully and trying to draw sustenance from them; an ordeal at first, no doubt, but calming to the spirit. Meredith also encouraged me to write plays, and sometimes when I was telling him of my characters, instead of commenting on their feebleness he would slip the paper-knife I have spoken of into my hand to stab them with, and even in great moments retain it and stab himself. There was Irving, too, who said I had such a 'kind' way of taking my characters 'off and on' that actors would always like to play them. It took me years to find out what this meant, but he at least had a kind way with me and 'placed' my first plays. Yet I preferred writing books, and still think they were more my game, and remain uncertain that those good friends did not do me a great disservice. What lured me on was that the writing was in dialogue, which fascinated me from the moment I fell into it and found that I could swim. It is a form that delights me still; to this day I even write many of my letters in it. I would preach in dialogue if I were a clergyman, and write my prescriptions in it if I were a physician.

In my first years, however, I never contemplated becoming a dramatist, and would have thought you harsh had you said it was the thing for me. No one would have been so astonished as Anon. The theatre and the oddities of its life drew me to them, but plays did not. I wrote papers as from an actor, as an actress, as a stage-door keeper, as one who runs tours, as a call-boy, as a dresser, but the playwright was to me the one uninteresting figure of the whole clamjamfry.

I seldom went to the play, though on the other hand I have always liked to sit alone in an empty theatre. At such times I have not planned scenarios, but I have thought out the novel of the stage I never wrote. At rehearsals, when they were esteeming me as amiable because I sat silent, I was far away in my book. I never knew (and I don't know now) how plays are written, nor gave stage-craft any conscious thought. It is strange to me to read of dramatists who in their beginnings go a score of times to see some popular play in order to study its construction. Nevertheless I have no doubt from what I hear and read that theirs is the better way. In an introduction I wrote to the plays of one of the best of us, now lying on French soil, I find that I began 'When I agreed very gladly to write a few words of introduction to this volume, I cautiously bought a book about how to write plays (there are many of them) in order to see whether Mr. Chapin wrote his plays properly; but the book was so learned, and the author knew so much, and the subject when studied grew so difficult that I hurriedly abandoned my inquiry.' My own plan was simply to make everything clear to myself in the hope that this would clear a way for the spectator. Once or twice I first made my clearing in the middle, as when I wrote the third act of

'The Admirable Crichton' before writing acts
one and two. I have not the least idea what
stage technique is, but this may have been it.
Plays should be 42 by 36. Let us admit this
and waywardly pass on.

As the dignified event now draws nigh which
must end our little book, this seems a fitting
moment to call again on Mr. Anon and ask him
for a record of his two years' travail. A Biblio-
graphy of his doings in this period finds some
seventy articles in the 'St. James's,' nearly all of
which, though they were of course unsigned, I
seem to recognize by their titles, though the very
skilful compiler, Mr. Herbert Garland, can have
had nothing to guide him save the British Museum
or ancient files. I know of as many more, so this
makes at least a hundred and forty accepted in
those two years. I am sure that far more than
twice that number had the sadder fate of rejection,
though the second year gave Anon much more
reason to rejoice than the first. Greenwood must
have had at least four hundred hurled at him by
the fast bowler, Anon. Those we have selected
are mainly from the first two years, because before
the end thereof Anon became, as we shall see, of
less importance to me. The bibliographer gives
a list of over two hundred such contributions used
by other journals in the second, third, and fourth

years, besides the many that still went to the 'St. James's.' He has no record of course of those declined. I think eight hundred is a mild estimate for Anon's four years. As there were also published by the end of the fourth year five books (some with a good deal of St. James's matter in them), 'Better Dead,' 'Auld Licht Idylls,' 'When a Man's Single,' 'An Edinburgh Eleven,' and 'A Window in Thrums,' they cannot be called four years of idleness. He was a humble atom was Mr. Anon, but I am glad he worked so hard.

One of his stand-by's was his friend Riach, editor of the 'Edinburgh Evening Dispatch,' but the man who altered all things for me, by admitting signed articles, was Robertson Nicoll of the 'British Weekly.' My first article for him (on Dr. Alexander Whyte, the famous Scottish divine) appeared on July 1, 1887, almost as important a date to me as that of fully two years earlier when the rooks began to build at St. Pancras Station. According to our bibliographer I wrote fifty or sixty articles for the 'British Weekly.' Nicoll also set me to the writing of books and got them published, and for the rest of his life was the wisest and kindest of counsellors; but the great thing he did for me was his putting an end to the anonymity, pushing Anon out and letting me in.

Farewell, Anon. You were not overworked in those strenuous years, nor except perhaps during the early months were you underfed. Soon (as it seems now) you got out of buns and cheese into luscious 'chips,' and so onward, ever onward, pertinacious soul, to chops and ale. Few freelances have been so fortunate as you, though you had your tremors. Your philosophy, so far as I can see through the mists, was to be always at it with your pen and let the skies fall if they chose. Would you have looked up, Anon? You knew not what was going on around you, nor apparently cared to know. To-day I read books about your times written by authors not then born, and yours is the blame if those books are novel and engrossing to me, as if they treated of strange happenings in foreign lands instead of about the London of which I was a part. You were in the throng of National Events and International Convulsions, vast Social Reforms, the rise and fall of Parties, Women were getting Ready, the Religion of the Prosperous had passed from Golf to Lawn Tennis, there were Balls and Jubilees and Junketings, there were Members in the Clock Tower, and you only noticed them as you looked up to dip. Your only concern with them was that if they crowded Oxford Street with processions you took your afternoon walk that day in the Euston Road among the monumental masons. How long were you wound up to go, Anon? Were you truly alive as you ticked away unheard? How long would your coat have been on fire before you noticed it? O spare and diligent crumb, I know that in those two years some sort of ecstasy was drumming in your minute inside, but I have forgotten what it was.

We had some good old miserable times together, hadn't we? Do you remember how we followed the postman from door to door, under the moon, in rain, in fog, to see him drop our fate into the letter-box or heartlessly go by? It fell as soft as pound notes when it was a proof, and like a damn when it was itself come back again. We may have had our discords, you and I, but can we ever forget that we sat as one on the box at St. Pancras Station? Wherever you now may be, wouldn't you for old times' sake rather listen to a rook than to a skylark?

I am glad it is I who ask the questions and not you who put them to me. I daresay you are curious about what happened after I edged you to the door. There was my grand ambition to do things instead of writing about them. Did I do them? No, Anon, I never did. To do something grandly perilous before settling down —was the phrase yours or mine? In your day it was to be Africa with Joseph Thomson, and later it was to be the Antarctic with Captain Scott, whom you never knew, but who was to become in after years my best of friends. A letter from him to me written in the tent in which he and his comrades died, is, I suppose, my most precious possession. No, I never went with either of them. You are right, it might have made a man of me. I suppose you are just as you were when Gilmour sketched you, but I question whether you would know me; gone lethargic, Anon, and indifferent, and walk with my staff behind my back, always a bad sign. You may ask me a question or two, though I don't promise to answer them. Grenville Street? No, I didn't stay on long after you had departed. The pound a day? Yes, I thought you would be curious about that. It goes on, Anon, and more; indeed it was more before you and I parted company. Gilmour, whom you called Gilray, what do you want to know about him? Ah yes, I remember now that you were still hanging around when Gilmour began to be so obstreperous about the cheques. When the cheques arrived like rich relations a change did come over me, Anon, and I was as reckless in money matters as you once were provident. In the end Gilmour got his way and I joined a Bank. He is my great friend still.

s

Surely there is one other thing you want to know about? Yes, the Hat. The Hat was yours rather than mine; it would sadden me if you did not want to know what became of the Hat. Well, the Bank did for the Hat. If you want to learn more about this curious matter read my remaining pages. You are already familiar with those that are about the Bank; they may indeed be called your last article, though the title is changed. I suppose it was you who went into the Bank that day and I who came out. What happened afterwards, however, will be new to you. Read it and then haste away from me. I love you in retrospect, but two years were quite enough of you. Go back to St. Pancras in the early morning and meet some new free-lance stepping from the train and be as helpful to him as you were to me. Begone, sweet Anon, begone.

CHAPTER XXIV

"FROM ST. PANCRAS TO THE BANK"

"I now proceed to tell how a literary hand opens a Bank Account. The requisites are recklessness tempered with stratagem, a devoted but maddened friend, time to elaborate your plot, an ingratiating manner, and cheques. I propose to show how the affair can be brought to a successful issue by describing my own adventures; and I may add as a guarantee of good faith that my cheque-book is lying before me as I write.

From the time my joining a bank was in contemplation until the scheme was hatched would be about three months. Long before this, however, my devoted friend Gilray and I had been closeted occasionally on the subject but without deciding on any line of action beyond the old one, namely, that I should continue giving him small crossed cheques, for which he should hand me as much cash as he could get for them. It was, if I remember aright, a hole in my waistcoat pocket that finally decided me to begin the practical proceedings. My devoted friend had got me sovereigns galore in exchange for some cheques, and they had gnawed a hole in my waistcoat pocket, through which they forced a way into the lining and ran round me like mice in a wall. To get at them I had to tilt myself to this side and that, much as we used to play the game of pigs in clover, and often (even in public places) with the same result—defeat at the sty. Instead of paying my creditors promptly, I had to invite them to listen while I gave myself a jerk. From this dilemma I proposed to extricate myself by following the now familiar arrangement of selling more cheques to my devoted friend; but though I had worried him successfully for long by appeals to his finer feelings, he finally rebelled, and said that as far as he was concerned I must open negotiations with a bank or starve. Of course he had me in his power, and I yielded, though with misgivings, for I have ever liked to go on in the old bad ways. We sat far on into various nights discussing which bank would be most easily duped, and other details. We finally decided to make our first attempt on a Bank several of the Directors of which were favourably known to him as not being good business men. He also consented to continue getting as much as possible for my cheques until we had outwitted the Banker. The scene of our plot, it is interesting to remember, was a house in Dash Street where I now resided in splendour, the room with the two windows.

For some weeks I did not see Gilray, and I began to hope that my momentary tangles were to go on in the old way. I also found an entry into the lining of my waistcoat, and, as a result, had the unwonted pleasure of asking all the persons I knew, except Gilray (whom I now scorned), to a festive function. Too soon I found myself impecunious, and had to write a begging letter to him offering some cheques at half price (for ready money). He gave me a paltry sum, but announced at the same time that it was the last, and that we must both now turn over a new leaf. He also said that the Bank (it was not his bank—he is a shrewd fellow) had consented (to oblige him) to let me open an account. This was the First Step. How he managed it I do not know; but during those three weeks he must have been working hard for me. He is well acquainted with Bankers, their ways, their vulnerable points, where to find them, when to strike and how to play them. It is astounding to hear him talk about stocks and shares and gold being up and down as easily as one could reel off an article. Though he seems, however, to have shown in this matter a knowledge of men (or rather of Bankers) that is almost gruesome, he

has his weak points like another, and by praising
his acumen I succeeded in wheedling him out
of one more tenner. I then ordered him to cease
talking about Bank Accounts, or to leave my
rooms.

He bided his time, and in another three weeks
I was in a condition to listen to what he (with
money in a box that had a lid to it) called reason.
We now approach Step Two towards opening a
Bank Account. I feared Step Two would mean
a great deal of anguish for me, such as going to
houses where I should meet the Directors, having
to take an unnerving lady in to dinner and being
asked financial posers. This made me anxious,
for my appearance is against me, and I take banks
like clubs, where the committees blackball all
candidates except those who are unknown to
them. (I am safe to be elected to the Athenæum.)
I pointed this out to Gilray, who was beginning
to show traces of arrogance, but he replied that
he had more sense than to let the Directors meet
me before they were too compromised to be able
to draw back. In short, Step Two had already
been taken without my cognizance. Step Three
(a very troublesome step this) was the arrangement of all my cheques one on top of another.
I put off taking this step as long as possible, and
then I made two steps of it; (*a*) consisted in

searching my envelopes, boxes, drawers, pockets and other likely places for cheques, of which I had a number, though all for small amounts. I had intentionally hidden them here and there, for one must be careful with cheques; (b) consisted in signing my name on the back of each. I then sallied forth in a fury to an eating-house where I had arranged to meet my devoted friend; thence after a light repast we were to proceed to the Bank. My devoted friend, finding that I had only got as far as (a) (a trick of mine to put off the visit to the Bank), insisted on our completing (b) in the restaurant. We therefore had our table cleared, by a stern order from Gilray who can awe the most majestic people, and proceeded to the orderly arrangement of the cheques amid breathless silence, the people at the other tables laying down their knives and forks, and the waiters gathering round us open-mouthed, as the pile grew bigger and its items tended to float. I wrote my name on the back of each of my cheques (this is compulsory), and then passed it to my Business Man, who made marks on a piece of paper. When all was over, he said there were fifty-two cheques. As I had made it fifty in the room with two windows we counted again, and this time we both found there were fifty-two. We then left the restaurant, the waiters looking

at us strangely.   It was now two o'clock, and the
sky a dull grey with moving clouds.   We have
now come to Step Four—the Bank itself.   As
we set off upon our singular adventure my mentor
may be conceived striding a little in front of me
and occasionally looking behind him.   Piccadilly
Circus was full of wayfarers, passing this way and
that.   Around us was the roar of traffic, above
us that grey sky with the clouds.   Strange to say,
as we neared the Bank in Pall Mall East it was
my friend who became the more despondent.
Perhaps mine was a Dutch courage; but it
served.   He murmured that Step Four would
perhaps make a miserly calculating man of me,
and that somehow he preferred me as I had
been.   If I wanted, he said, to go on in the old
harum-scarum way, there was still time.   But
I clenched my teeth, and into the Bank
we marched.

Have you ever been in a bank?   I had only
time to glance furtively around me when we were
shown into a small room.   The door was quickly
closed, and we were alone with the Bankers.   My
first reflection was that the window could not be
more than five feet from the ground.   Then I
saw that Gilray was introducing me to the
Bankers.   Bankers are of medium height, slightly
but firmly built, forty or forty-one years of age,

and stand in an easy attitude, with nothing about them to suggest their vocation save that they keep their hands in their trouser-pockets. They have pleasant voices, but you do not catch what they say, and all that is expected of you is to bow when they have completed a sentence. You also hand over your cheques and sign your name twice on different pieces of paper, so as to give them some sort of a pull over you, and then after a last look at you which is rather trying, they hand you your cheque-book. Cheque-books are in blue covers and are of a shape which makes them wobble in the hand like a trout.

At this moment, which should have been the 'crowning moment,' everything threatened to go plop, for they began to talk to each other on everyday topics, leaving me out of it, and the idiotic Gilray, losing his head, collected his hat and stick. They probably saw from my face that I was not to be trifled with, and presently one asked with assumed lightness whether I would like anything now, and if so how much. I said firmly that I should like ten pounds (in gold); and I got it too, without their knowing I would have closed with them if they had said that five would be more convenient. I soon wished that I had tried them with fifteen. I did all this myself without the least help from Gilray, and then I made off quickly in a cab, dropping him carelessly at his home, for I had no further need of him.

Though you must already see that a Bank Account is a good thing to scheme for, I have not yet shown how useful it is. The ten pounds referred to is not (as those without banking knowledge may assume) all I got for my fifty-two cheques. When it was exhausted, I went back to the Bank, taking care to go immediately after I thought the officials had lunched (that I might catch them in a knightly mood). I fixed on the youngest Cashier, and in a devil-may-care sort of way, but without a word, I slipped a cheque beneath his rail. It was an anxious moment. 'Gold or notes?' he asked. 'Gold,' I said calmly. (Always be careful to say gold.) The next time I doubled the sum and got it again. I never pay for anything now, I give cheques instead. I sometimes feel that this cannot last, for I have no hold on the Bank, and some day doubtless they will find out something damaging to me in those two signatures I gave them. While it lasts, however, I know nothing equal to a Bank Account. No literary hand should be without one."

ENVOI

GOOD-BYE TO THE HAT

THAT is how it was, except of course that Gilmour's services had consisted in exchanging cheques with me; as he was such a good friend I naturally wanted in the article to put him in the worst light. The restaurant was the Monico and the bank Barclay's branch in Pall Mall East. I am not sure that the sky was a dull grey, but the rest is accurate. I chanced to hear afterwards that Tennyson had read the account aloud at a garden party, and this naturally pleased me and pleases me still.

Thus, however, ends the Hat. Unless the gentle reader is dull in the uptake he will not need to be told why. As soon as you have a bank account you no longer need to have a silk hat. To cut any considerable dash in London as a free-lance you must have one or the other, but it is a mark of the pretentious to have both. Such at least was my feeling, and though I continued to visit my Greenwood it was henceforth in a billycock. I was grateful for all the Hat had done for me, but relieved to be able to return it

283

to its box, whence it has long since flown, I know
not whither. I should like to think that Anon
balances it once more on his head as good-luck
to the newcomer whom he is awaiting at St.
Pancras. I referred to it in the following words
at a great dinner given to Greenwood in the
year 1907 (with a bunch of violets from Mr.
Meredith), when I for that occasion made a last
reappearance as Anon:—

'I dare not say in public how much I love
Mr. Greenwood. He invented me. I owe
almost everything to him. I bought my first
silk hat to impress him the day I came to London.
I never wore it except when I made my periodic
advances upon the "St. James's." I like to think
that it had its effect on him. There was a legend
that he could not smoke a cigar without putting
a pen-nib through it, and that he preferred your
pen-nib. I do not know whether his immediate
neighbours, Mr. Morley and Mr. Asquith and
Lord Crewe, have pens with them this evening,
but if so they are no longer the pens they were.
I was only a free-lance, but once I had a sublime
week of assisting in that newspaper office, and
Mr. Greenwood's cigars turned my attention to
smoking. I did not smoke in those days, I
abominated the practice, but my game was to
study his weaknesses, and so I took to writing

favourably on that topic. I wrote so many articles about my lady nicotine (who was really his lady) that I made a book of them. Long afterwards I read the book and was so fascinated by its pictures of the delights of tobacco that I took to smoking. If I were writing a guide to London I would put three stars to the name of Greenwood. There are many others of us, a whole line of anonymous Tom Smiths passing in their first silk hat, the Greenwood Hat. In honour to-night of the Beginner's Friend we take off every hat we ever had; but, O Greenwood, it is because of those first silk hats that we love you best. They are old and battered now, but dying they salute you.'